AMERICA IN THE 21ST CENTURY: POLITICAL AND ECONOMIC ISSUES

CORPORATE GOVERNANCE AND THE U.S. FIRM: A REVIEW AND DIRECTIONS FOR FUTURE RESEARCH

DINA FAISAL EL-MAHDY
AND
CAROLYN STRAND NORMAN

Nova Science Publishers, Inc.
New York

For permission to use material from this book please contact us:
Telephone 631-231-7269; Fax 631-231-8175
Web Site: http://www.novapublishers.com

LIBRARY OF CONGRESS CATALOGING-IN-PUBLICATION DATA

Norman, Carolyn Strand.
Corporate governance and the firm : a review and directions for future research / Carolyn Strand Norman and Dina Faisal El-Mahdy.
p. cm.
Includes index.
ISBN 978-1-61728-782-4 (hardcover)
1. Corporate governance--United States. 2. Corporations--Accounting. 3. Corporations--Research. I. El-Mahdy, Dina Faisal. II. Title.
HD2741.N85 2010
338.60973--dc22-2010026982

Published by Nova Science Publishers, Inc. New York

AMERICA IN THE 21ST CENTURY: POLITICAL AND ECONOMIC ISSUES

CORPORATE GOVERNANCE AND THE U.S. FIRM: A REVIEW AND DIRECTIONS FOR FUTURE RESEARCH

AMERICA IN THE 21ST CENTURY: POLITICAL AND ECONOMIC ISSUES

Additional books in this series can be found on Nova's website under the Series tab.

Additional E-books in this series can be found on Nova's website under the E-books tab.

CONTENTS

ACKNOWLEDGMENTS

We thank each and every scholar whose research work is cited in this book. These scholarly works enhanced our understanding of the usefulness of corporate governance and helped us in shaping our recommendations.

Preface

In the past, corporate governance was an important control mechanism for maintaining the accountability of management and directors of an organization. However, the value of strong corporate governance has assumed a critical role in organizations since recent highly publicized business failures of a number of large companies. Claims about the unreliability of reported earnings continue, as evidenced by an increase in the frequency of earnings restatements, earnings management, and fraud. Thus, corporate governance systems continue to be of utmost importance based on the impact of financial reporting (e.g., firm value, earnings and audit quality, firm performance) on capital markets. This book provides a comprehensive review, discussion, and analysis of over 150 research works on the usefulness of corporate governance codes to U.S. firms based on theory underlying corporate governance, anecdotal evidence, and practices. The book first introduces the multi-faceted aspects of corporate governance, reviews corporate governance codes and their unplanned consequences on U.S. firms, and then classifies the extant literature on corporate governance over the last two decades, from 1990 to 2010. The book further discusses the association between corporate governance and organizational outcomes such as firm value, performance, and financial reporting quality to draw conclusions regarding the overall effectiveness of corporate governance codes to U.S. firms. Based on this classification, the book offers directions for future research regarding corporate governance mechanisms to maximize their benefit to U.S. firms.

This book is motivated by the extensive literature on corporate governance that attempts to answer the question: what is the value of corporate governance to U.S. firms? The authors also note that research on corporate governance in business, finance, economics, management, and accounting is widespread and continues due to the struggles (and in some cases, collapse) of major firms worldwide, following the global financial crisis in 2007-2008, even though most of these firms have strong governance structures. Moreover, most of these wide-ranging studies lack evidence on the systematic usefulness of corporate governance to different constituencies, especially to firm value, performance, and financial reporting quality. The debate is interesting yet still unresolved by academics as to whether corporate governance did add value to the U.S. firm. There is also doubt in the literature that there is an agreement between theoretical frameworks of corporate governance provided by the literature and the best corporate governance practices employed by corporations. Accordingly, our book attempts to provide this missing link by offering a comprehensive review of the usefulness of corporate governance to U.S. firms.

The authors find that articulating the empirical evidence with the theoretical foundations underpinning corporate governance codes is essential to our understanding of the overall effect of corporate governance systems to U.S. firms. We then set the stage for future research that would advance knowledge of the value of corporate governance. This book may be used for teaching, research, and/or professional reference, and should be of interest to a wide variety of audiences, such as: graduate students who conduct research on corporate governance in the business disciples, including accounting, finance, law, and management; professors who either conduct research on corporate governance or teach graduate students a course on corporate governance; professors who teach executive MBA courses, boards of directors, governance committees; as well as management in public firms, professional bodies that set governance codes and regulations (e.g., SEC, FASB, IASB and PACOB), practitioners such as auditors, tax experts, and financial analysts who apply corporate governance codes in their day-to-day activities. Our book focuses on directly linking practice and theory in the extant empirical and experimental research on the association between corporate governance and organizational outcomes, which is a missing link in current corporate governance books. Our book also provides a comprehensive overview on how successful corporate governance is to U.S. firms. Most importantly, we provide directions for future research based on the content of corporate governance research over the last two decades.

This book is comprised of five parts. Part one discusses the multi-faceted aspects of corporate governance codes in the U.S.. Part one is composed of three chapters. Chapter one defines corporate governance, the reasons for corporate governance, and how corporate governance works. In addition, chapter one comprehensively lists corporate governance mechanisms, both internal and external, that are considered best practices for corporate governance. Chapter two introduces the most cited underlying theories for corporate governance, such as agency theory, resource dependence theory, stakeholders' theory, contingent theory, and others. Chapter three provides background about the Sarbanes Oxley Act of 2002 (hereafter SOX 2002). Chapter three further lists the most significant SOX 2002 provisions and some unpredictable consequences on firm value and performance.

Part two discusses corporate governance and U.S. firm performance. It is composed of three chapters. Chapter four reviews and classifies the literature on corporate governance and stock price performance. Chapter five focuses on the association between corporate governance and firm operating performance measures, such as return on equity and Tobin's Q. Chapter six discusses corporate governance and internal control material weaknesses pre- and post-SOX 2002, as well as SOX 2002 provisions related to internal control material weaknesses, such as sections 302 and 404.

In the same vein, part three of this book discusses and summarizes the literature on the association between corporate governance and financial reporting quality. Part three is composed of three chapters (from chapter seven to chapter nine). Chapter seven introduces the definition and importance of financial reporting quality to the firm and hence reviews the literature on corporate governance and earnings management with emphasize on the conflicting two points of view on whether corporate governance curbs or does not curb earnings management practices. Corporate governance and analysts' forecasts are the main subjects of chapter eight. Chapter nine covers the effect of corporate governance on the audit profession including, but is not limited to, audit quality, process, fees, tenure, and resignation.

An overview of a sample of research on the association between corporate governance and non-U.S. firms is summarized in part four. In this part, the authors classify the international evidence into various categories that relate non-U.S. firm value and performance to corporate governance best practices.

Part five concludes our book by recommending directions or guidelines for future research based on the theoretical, anecdotal, and empirical evidence discussed in earlier chapters. Part five is composed of three chapters (from chapter eleven to chapter thirteen). In chapter eleven, the authors propose studying the proactive role of corporate governance in the global financial crisis. Chapter twelve discusses the available meta analysis research in corporate governance and how to get the most out of meta analysis methodology as guidance for future research. Other recommendations for future research are the main topics of chapter thirteen in which we discuss the importance of studying the antecedents, characteristics, and consequences of corporate governance endogenous structure, the importance of working on corporate governance convergences, utilizing psychological theories in empirical corporate governance research, documenting corporate governance codes in U.S. history, the benefits of incorporating eXtensible Business Reporting Language (XBRL) into corporate governance codes, and others.

PART I: CORPORATE GOVERNANCE AND U.S. FIRMS

Chapter 1

WHAT IS CORPORATE GOVERNANCE AND BEST GOVERNANCE PRACTICES?

WHAT IS CORPORATE GOVERNANCE?

Corporate governance has variously been defined as the processes, ethics, policies, guidelines, and rules that firms adopt to reduce agency costs arising from the conflict of interest between the management (agent) and shareholders (principal) of organizations. This conflict of interest arises mainly from the unique nature of the dispersed ownership structure that separates ownership of capital and management of control over this capital. Unlike the concentrated ownership systems such as those in Germany and Japan, the U.S. system is characterized as a dispersed ownership system with significant distance between management and shareholders. The increased emphasize on corporate governance in the U.S. stems from the fact that the U.S. is currently the world's richest and largest dispersed ownership system (Anglo-American). However, such a system gives rise to certain problems, which encouraged regulators to mandate a strong corporate governance system in publicly-traded companies. The U.S. is also a contractarian system in which the primary purpose of the firm is to maximize the shareholders' (residual claimants) value.

In the corporate governance domain, the primary groups involved are management, board of directors, and shareholders of a firm. However, other interested parties might include customers, suppliers, bond holders, regulators, and other stakeholders. Traditionally, shareholders delegate their rights to the management of a firm to act on their behalf but shareholders are usually unable to directly monitor the actions of management. Likewise, managers' primary interest is to maximize the firm's profits to maximize their bonus and compensation plans. Jensen and Meckling (1976) theorize the conflict of interest between managers and shareholders this way: *"Manages who own less than 100% of the residual cash flow rights of the firm are more than likely to have a potential conflict of interest with the firm's shareholders".* Therefore, there is a mismatch between the interest of management and shareholders and this mismatch creates information asymmetry. This information asymmetry between managers and shareholders provides the underlying need for corporate governance codes.

WHY DOES CORPORATE GOVERNANCE EXIST?

Why does Corporate Governance exist? In other words, what creates a conflict of interest between management and shareholders that mandates the existence of corporate governance? First, we will consider the interest of each group and second we will pinpoint the gap that initiates this conflict of interest. On one hand, the shareholders are commonly interested in the financial outcomes of the firm expressed as the positive dollar amount resulting from the net operating activities of the firm. As the firm achieves positive income, shareholders' wealth goes up in terms of either share repurchases or dividends on their stocks. Otherwise, managers might retain those earnings in the firm for future expansion or investment in profitable projects to maximize that positive income in the future. To the extent that managers are not doing their due diligence and are not giving their best efforts to maximize firm profits, shareholders' wealth might deteriorate. Since management is expected to act as an agent on behalf of shareholders, agency costs might initiate. On the other hand, managers do not own the stocks of the firm; they are entrusted to manage the ownership of stocks. However, management is said to be mostly interested in power, recognition, and compensation. In other words, managers want to remain in their jobs as the team leaders of the firm and sometimes they overlook the fact that their position carries responsibility rather than power. Management might seek recognition and this might lead to high costs associated with this recognition. Management also seeks high compensation and bonuses; therefore, managers have a tendency to achieve short-term profits to maximize their compensation in the short run. These diverse managerial interests are not in line with those of the various shareholders' interests of a firm. Here comes the conflict of interest between managers and shareholders that usually results in high agency costs due to the need for monitoring managerial actions. From this conflict-of-interest perspective, agency theory was developed to describe the need to align the interest of managers with those of shareholders and various stakeholders to minimize agency costs. Moreover, the recent corporate failures of worldwide firms renewed the interest in strong corporate governance in an effort to restore the trust of investors in the market.

Denis (2001) suggests three solutions to reduce the agency problem and hence costs associated with it. These solutions center on aligning the interests of managers with those of their shareholders to bridge the gap between these two conflicting interests. That is, tie managers contractually, monitor managers, or provide incentives to managers that would align managements' interests to those of shareholders. A contracting solution requires managers to sign a contract stating that they will act in a manner that maximizes shareholders wealth. Monitoring solutions include the issuance of corporate governance codes such as SOX 2002. An example of incentive-alignment solutions to the conflict of interest between management and shareholders would be managerial bonus and compensation plans that tend to be set in line with the shareholders' objectives (e.g., profit maximization). To the extent that contracting or incentives plans are not effective in reducing agency costs and/or fail to align the interests of management with those of shareholders, corporate governance codes might act as a monitoring tool over managerial performance and actions.

In summary, the transaction or agency cost that arises from the mismatch of interests between management and stakeholders is what initiates the need for effective corporate governance monitoring tools. This transaction or agency cost is usually not mitigated through the regular contracts between management and stakeholders. This transaction cost also cannot be avoided due to the ambiguity and information asymmetry between management and shareholders. Therefore, corporate governance may be the critical mechanism that helps reduce transaction or agency costs.

How does Corporate Governance Work?

What can be done to align the interest of management with those of shareholders? An important step to align the interests of management with those of shareholders is to allow shareholders access to truthful, credible, and up-to-date information about firm performance on a regular basis. Firm information is traditionally transmitted by management to firms' shareholders via public disclosure of periodic financial reporting of the firm to market-wide participants. To the extent that management knows more private information than shareholders do, an information asymmetry between management and shareholders exists. This information asymmetry is costly because it allows one party to gain abnormal returns from foreknowledge of private information relative to others. To alleviate this information asymmetry and its associated costs, management would need to seek ways to deliver information about the firm to shareholders. The cost of providing this information to shareholders is described as agency cost, and includes auditor's fees to verify the truthfulness of the financial reports of the firm, credit rating agencies fees, the cost of providing the information to financial analysts, and the cost of corporate governance itself (such as the costs of attracting independent outside directors on the board of directors). Corporate governance can improve the quality of information transmitted from management to shareholders by forcing management to take the necessary steps to provide credible, transparent, timely, and accurate information that correctly describes the financial position of the firm at a specific time. In fact, corporate governance can achieve economic equilibrium in a firm in the sense that it makes the agency cost of monitoring the management equal to the profits from the reduction that arises from management's expropriation (e.g., consumption of perquisites and shirking) of shareholders' wealth.

BEST CORPORATE GOVERNANCE PRACTICES

Theoretically, in the U.S., the best corporate governance practices are mainly those set forth by the Sarbanes Oxley Act of 2002, the Securities and Exchange Commission, and other regulatory agencies such as the Public Company Accounting Oversight Board (PCAOB). The primary objective of these governance regulations is to promote the most efficient governance structure. Such a structure is supposed to help curb fraud and financial problems associated with information asymmetry between shareholders and management.

In general, corporate governance best practices can be divided into two broad mechanisms: external and internal mechanisms (Bushman and Smith 2001). External corporate control mechanisms consist of the market for corporate control, the external managerial labor market, the national legal and judicial system, and product market competition. Internal corporate control mechanisms include managerial incentives plans, shareholders and debt holders monitoring, board monitoring, corporate bylaws and charters, and the internal managerial labor market. Farinha (2003); Shleifer and Vishny (1997); Jensen and Meckling (1976); and Bushman and Smith (2001) among others discuss these two broad groups of corporate governance mechanisms.

Some of the best governance practices focus on disciplining external parties (e.g., the external auditor) as an influential factor in achieving the equilibrium of agency costs. For example, according to the best governance practices set by SOX 2002, auditors are prohibited from providing non-audit services to maintain their independence. Among the governance mechanisms that contribute to aligning the interest of managers with those of shareholders is the allocation of ownership between insiders and outsiders, the use of debt in the capital structure to reduce the free cash flow that can be abused by management, managerial incentive plans, takeover, board of directors, investor activisms, product market competition, and organizational structure (Farinha, 2003).

Overall, theory and practice suggest that certain internal governance practices, if followed, will provide benefits to the firm. The best governance practices in the academic literature have been heavily focusing on the board of directors and the formulations of various independent governance committees by the board of directors. Therefore, the existence, independence, structure, and composition of the governance committees are among the best governance practices in the literature. Corporate Governance committees include nominating committees, compensation committees, and audit committees.

In this section, we discuss these governance mechanisms. In the next chapters, we provide empirical evidence on the usefulness of these best governance mechanisms to firm value, performance, and financial reporting quality.

External Corporate Governance Mechanisms

External governance mechanisms include the corporate hostile takeover or takeover threat, product market competition, managerial labor market, financial analysts, the legal environment, and management reputation. Some argue that market competition, as a governance tool, takes too much time to come up with positive tangible outcomes regarding the value of a firm. This section lists the external corporate governance mechanisms discussed in prior scholarly research.

Hostile Takeover or Takeover Threat

In a typical takeover situation, management is not maximizing shareholders' wealth, and therefore loses the trust of shareholders. Consequently, a firm can be acquired by the management of another firm, which fixes the problems created by the old management, and then the new management can sell the firm for a higher price at a later date. However, as simple as it might sound, a corporate takeover is usually very costly (e.g., bidding and transaction costs), yet it is considered an important external corporate governance mechanism. Anecdotal evidence suggests that a takeover is associated with higher stock market prices for the target firm and synergistic gains from the merger process. Sometimes the hostile takeover is not as effective as is the takeover *threat*. This is because the takeover threat attempts to threaten the current management of a possible takeover if the current management does not perform its due diligence in maximizing the shareholders wealth. Usually, the takeover threat does not entail high costs, unlike that of the hostile takeover. Therefore, the takeover threat achieves the target of disciplining management with minimal costs.

Product Market Competition

Evidence suggests that natural forces of market competition help mitigate managerial expropriation of shareholders' wealth. However, product market competition works only in a free (efficient) market where there are no monopolistic firms. It is also worthwhile to note that product market competition takes too much time to establish market equilibrium to correct the potential hazard of management expropriation of shareholders' wealth.

Managerial Labor Market

Managers' performance and hence their estimated level of pay by the market could be determined from the performance of the firm they manage. Hence, managerial labor market natural forces may be used as an external corporate governance mechanism. Labor market forces incorporate not only a current firm's performance of the managers but also the history of the firm's performance. Managers are more likely to work on maximizing a firm's profit and shareholders' wealth if the top management team's compensations are a reflection of that effort. Hence, managers are expected to align their interests with those of the firm in order to increase the weight of managerial compensations and wages in the market.

Financial Analysts, Banks, Brokerages, and Institutional Investors

Financial analysts, banks, brokerages, and institutional investors play an important role in disciplining management of firms due to their oversight role. Financial analysts, banks, brokerage, and institutional investors monitor firm performance and report estimates of a firm's future earnings based on the financial analysts' expectations of a firm's performance. Thus, management is mindful of financial analysts' opinions. Management of a firm typically attempt to "beat" or "exceed" financial analysts' expectations in order to surprise the market with favorable news, which is then incorporated in the firm's stock returns and market capitalizations. This favorable market news is usually observable in higher shareholders' value. As a result, financial analysts may be considered an external corporate governance mechanism that helps align the interests of management with those of shareholders and hence reduces agency costs.

The Legal Environment

The legal environment includes Federal and state regulations and legislation that attempt to curb aggressive managerial behavior which in turn diminishes shareholders' wealth. Examples of these controls include the Securities and Exchange Commission rules to encourage shareholder activism in 1990 and SOX 2002 in the U.S., as well as the Cadbury code issued in 1992 in the UK. Although the legal system is theoretically considered an influential mechanism in setting market-wide rules to protect shareholders' wealth, Jensen (1993) argues that the legal system is: *"far too blunt an instrument to handle the problems of wasteful managerial behavior effectively"*. Therefore, we report literature that focuses on both the legal environment and firm-level governance variables that may be considered external corporate governance tools.

Management Reputation

Managers and executives are interested in power, recognition, and reputation. One way to maintain a prestigious managerial reputation in the market is to manage a firm efficiently and effectively, thus building a good firm reputation in the market. Accordingly, a manager's interests would be in line with shareholders' interests if a manager is concerned about his/her reputation in the labor market. From this perspective, management reputation is considered an external corporate governance mechanism. However, one may anticipate that managerial reputation in the market is not of equal importance to all managers. That is, managerial reputation may be easily offset by other managerial motives, such as maximizing compensation and bonus plans in the short term, and gaining the power and recognition they desire from the firm. Due to these conflicting points of view, managerial reputation has not gained attention in the literature as an important external corporate governance mechanism. That is, management reputation appears to have a weak effect on reducing agency costs.

Internal Corporate Governance Mechanisms

Internal corporate governance mechanisms include: shareholder activism, the firm's board of directors, insider ownership, compensation packages, capital structure, and dividends. In this section, we discuss each of these governance tools and the philosophy underlying each one.

Shareholder Activism

In 1990, the SEC issued a provision to allow shareholders to engage in shareholder activism efforts. This provision allows shareholders who have less than a 5% holding in the firm to be able to communicate with other shareholders in the firm. Prior to 1990, the shareholder had to have a holding of more than 10% of the firm to be able to communicate with other shareholders. As a result, the 1990 provision was the beginning of stronger corporate governance mechanisms, because more institutional investors are allowed to monitor a firm's executives, and are also allowed to participate in shareholder activism efforts, which helps to efficiently monitor managerial actions and firm performance. Moreover, anecdotal evidence suggests that shareholder activism is in most cases associated with higher stock prices in the period surrounding shareholders' activism, implying that the market considers this action good news which will positively impact the future performance of the firm. Large shareholders' activism is also a signal (takeover threat) from shareholders to the current management that a hostile takeover is a distinct possibility. On the other hand, large shareholders' activism might initiate another source of conflict and agency costs. That is, shareholders' activism could result in two groups of shareholders: a controlled group (large shareholders) and a minority group (outsider shareholders) and these two groups may need corporate governance mechanisms that align their interests in the same direction.

In a review of the corporate finance literature on the effect of institutional investors' activities on corporate governance, Romano (2005) investigates the effect of confidential voting proposals on voting outcomes and concludes that activism has little or no effect on targeted firms' performance. Thus, she suggests that activist institutions should reassess their agenda to use resources more effectively. This might be accomplished by (1) engaging in periodic reviews of shareholder-activism programs to identify the most fruitful governance objectives, and (2) eliminating or significantly reducing the subsidy of proposal sponsorship under the Securities and Exchange Commission rules unless a proposal achieved substantial voting support.

Related, Shleifer and Vishny (1997) claim that if legal protection does not give enough control and rights to small investors, then perhaps investors can obtain more effective control rights by being large. When control rights are concentrated in the hands of a small number of investors with a collectively large cash flow stake, concerted action by investors is much easier than when control rights, such as votes, are split among many of them. According to Shleifer and Vishny's (1997) survey, a minority shareholder has the incentive to collect information, to monitor management, to put pressure on management, or in some cases, to exile management through a proxy fight or a takeover. A particular mechanism for consolidating ownership has emerged, namely, the hostile takeover, in which a bidder makes a tender offer to the dispersed shareholders of the target firm, and if they accept this offer, acquires control of the target firm and can replace, or at least control, management of the firm. Takeovers can thus be viewed as a mechanism for ownership concentration. Moreover, Shleifer and Vishny (1997) claim that U.S. shareholders and creditors are considered the most legally protected groups (from expropriation by managers) in the world. They further claim that the real conflict of interest in large corporations exists from the conflict of interest between large controlling shareholders and outside investors. A shareholder who owns 5% or more of the firm's common stock is generally a large shareholder or a blockholder. This possession of large ownership by a shareholder gives him/her the right to monitor the firm's activity.

Similarly, Gillan and Starks (2000) assess the effectiveness of shareholder activism by institutional and individual investors in the U.S. They use 2042 shareholder proposals submitted by 452 companies from 1987 to 1994. Two measures of the effectiveness of shareholder activism are used: the voting outcomes on the proxy proposals and the stock market reaction to the proposals. The results of the study suggest that shareholder voting and stock market reaction depend on the issues addressed by the proposals that were submitted, as well as the identity of the proposal sponsor. Proposals sponsored by active individual investors earned fewer votes and were associated with a slight positive impact on stock prices. On the other hand, proposals sponsored by institutional investors (such as pension funds) received more votes and had a small but measurable negative impact on stock prices.

In the same vein, Turnbull (1997) argues that institutional investors own more than half the top U.S. firms and this in fact intensifies agency problems. A typical example of large shareholders or blockholders is mutual trusts or fund managers who usually own and control large blocks of stocks in various firms. Large shareholders or blockholders have the incentive and ability to monitor management actions and help align the interests of management with those of shareholders. However, the key issue is that mutual funds and pensions which constitute the majority of institutional investors are run by agents such as fiduciary agents (Fan, 2004), who are dealing with agents of the top U.S. firms on a regular basis. When agents protect the shareholders rights against expropriation by other agents, the chances of incurring agency costs increase. Therefore, large shareholders, in some instances, can increase rather than decrease agency costs.

Board of Directors

The board of directors is elected by the shareholders of a firm. The board of directors plays three main roles in the firm: control/monitoring, service, and research dependence. Nevertheless, we note a predominant focus on the control/monitoring role of the board of directors in the literature. The board of directors' main task is to monitor the activity of top management in order to prevent the management from expropriating shareholders' wealth. In doing so, the board of directors is expected to hire, fire, and determine both the structure and level of compensation for the top management executives. Therefore, corporate governance codes focus on the board of directors as an important mechanism for aligning the interests of shareholders and management. The focus on the board of directors in the literature has ranged from merely discussing what would be the best board characteristics that achieve corporate governance objectives to extensive investigation of the significance of the board characteristics that are claimed to be the best governance practices. These board characteristics include board size, expertise, tenure, number of meetings, number of directorships, composition (e.g., insiders versus outsiders), independence, structure, the credibility of the board who wears many hats (dual directors/CEO) and whether the board receives fees in terms of stock or cash.

Governance mechanisms using the board of directors also include imposing age and term limits for directors, and imposing compensation package conditions that tie pay to firm performance for executives. Research suggests that the best governance practices will be attained when the board of directors is mostly composed of independent outsiders, is composed of a reasonable number of directors (board size), is separated from the chairman of the firm, and is prevented from interlocking directorates (where managers of two companies serve on each other's board to either protect their interest as a social elite group or to fulfill the resources needed by these two companies). Theory suggests that boards comprised mostly of insiders are assumed to align the interests of management with their desired interests (e.g., quality of financial reporting according to management preferences), which hinders the boards' oversight and monitoring function over the management. This in turn could increase the likelihood of earnings management, accounting restatements, internal control material weaknesses, perhaps fraud, and the expropriation of shareholders' wealth by management. On the other hand, the higher the number of outsiders on the board increases board independence from management and would presumably help achieve more favorable outcomes to shareholders, including higher quality financial reporting, reduced agency costs, more effective internal control, and higher firm profitability and market value. Research has also tested the frequency with which the board of directors meets and argues that the number of board meetings can be used as an internal corporate governance mechanism. In addition, prior research investigates the board of directors' diversity, and argues that having a board of different ethnicity, race, background, expertise, and nationality brings a relatively higher value to the firm than non-diversified board of directors.

Research on the effectiveness of governance mechanisms, using the board of directors, is numerous and surprisingly provides mixed results. These mixed results are due to the fact that the board of directors is a *dynamic* governance tool that is endogenously related to firm value. We will discuss research on the association between board of directors and firm performance in part two of this book.

Insider Ownership

Another source of internal corporate governance mechanisms is to increase the managerial stock ownership in the firm. However, this can be a very sensitive two-sided tool because the effect ranges from being an incentive that aligns the interests of management with shareholders to being an entrenchment that protects management from external corporate governance disciplining mechanisms. Theoretically speaking, if management owns part of a firm's stock, they will work for the interests of shareholders because they share the same interests as shareholders. Yet, as Adam Smith pointed out in his famous book *The Wealth of Nations*, managers need to own 100% of the company's stock to fully mitigate agency costs. Therefore, with anything less that 100% ownership, managers will not be completely motivated to align their interests with those of shareholders. In fact, managers might aggressively expropriate shareholders' wealth by trading on the firm's private information to gain abnormal returns.

Even when managers own some stock in the firm they manage, information asymmetry still exists between management and shareholders. For example, managers can make a trade off between the benefits they gain from maximizing shareholders' wealth and the costs they might incur from expropriating shareholders' wealth. Stated differently, managers will likely choose actions that will yield higher short-term profits to maximize their compensation and bonus packages. There is also evidence that managers of a firm trade their holdings of firm stocks based on their private information, and as a result, have been sued by the SEC[1].

[1] For more information on the litigation releases by the SEC, please check this link: http://www.sec.gov/divisions/enforce/friactions.shtml

Another problem associated with insider ownership as a corporate governance tool is the concept of managerial entrenchment. Managerial entrenchment is defined as a situation where managers are essentially protected from external corporate governance disciplining forces such as: product market competition, managerial labor market, and takeover threat. Managerial entrenchment normally occurs when management controls the majority of voting rights inside the firm and, as a result, can determine the destiny of the firm (e.g., future takeover actions, dispensing cash flow in a way that deteriorates shareholders' wealth and maximizes management wealth instead). Consequently, one can conclude that insider ownership as a corporate governance mechanism has both advantages and disadvantages.

Compensation Packages

Compensation and bonus packages (e.g., stock options, cash compensation, dividends) allegedly reduce agency costs and align the interests of management with those of shareholders. However, empirical evidence does not support this view. In practice, compensation packages are not literally tied to firm performance and shareholders' maximization of wealth. Overall, research suggests that compensation packages alone do not mitigate agency costs but may be used in conjunction with other corporate governance mechanisms to achieve effective oversight of management behavior.

Capital Structure

The balance between the dollar value of shareholders' equity versus those of debtholders helps align the interests of managers with those of shareholders of a firm. More specifically, debt rather than equity can be used as an internal corporate governance instrument. Managers who must deal with debt contracts are more likely to devote available cash flow to the repayment of debt and its associated costs (e.g., interest rates). Moreover, debt contracts are sometimes associated with financial debt covenants and collateral which put some restrictions on management and require a certain level of firm performance. As the penalty of violating these financial debt covenants increases, management will tend to maximize firm performance and, by default, shareholders' wealth will increase. Therefore, debt has been viewed in the literature as an important corporate governance mechanism.

Dividends

Anecdotal evidence suggests that dividends increase the likelihood that the firm's stock will be traded in the capital markets. As a result, in a firm that consistently declares dividends, institutional investors, banks, security analysts, and market participants will be motivated to examine the firm's performance and assess management's ability to maximize shareholders' wealth. Therefore, a firm's dividend policy has been considered in the literature as an internal corporate governance monitoring tool over the management of a firm.

REFERENCES

Bushman, R., and Smith, A. 2001. Financial accounting information and corporate governance. *Journal of Accounting & Economics* 32: 237-333.

Denis, D. 2001. Twenty-five years of corporate governance research…and counting. *Review of Financial Economics* 10: 191-212.

Fan, P. 2004. Review of literature and empirical research on corporate governance. *The Monetary Authority of Singapore Staff Paper No. 29.*

Farinha, J. 2003. Corporate governance: A survey of the literature. *Universidade do Porto Economia Discussion Paper No. 2003-06.* Available at SSRN: http://ssrn.com/abstract=470801 or doi:10.2139/ssrn.470801.

Gillan, S. and Starks, L. 2000. Corporate governance proposals and shareholder activism: The role of institutional investors. *Journal of Financial Economics* 57: 275-305.

Jensen, M. 1993. The modern industrial revolution, exit, and the failure of internal control systems. *Journal of Finance* 48: 831–880.

______ , and Meckling, W. 1976. Theory of the firm: Managerial behavior, agency costs and ownership structure. *Journal of Financial Economics* 3: 305–360.

Romano, R. 2005. The Sarbanes-Oxley Act and the making of quack corporate governance. *Yale Law Journal* 114: 1521–1611.

Shleifer, A. and Vishny, R. 1997. A survey of corporate governance. *The Journal of Finance* 2: 737-783.

Smith, A. 1776. The Wealth of Nations. Edited by Edwin Cannan, 1904. Reprint edition 1937. New York, Modern Library.

Turnbull, S. 1997. Corporate Governance: its scope, concerns and theories. *Corporate Governance* 5 (4): 180-206.

Chapter 2

CORPORATE GOVERNANCE UNDERLYING THEORIES

In this chapter, we discuss the most cited corporate governance theories in the literature. We find that agency theory is the prominent theory underlying corporate governance codes; however, we also find other competing theories such as: Contingency Theory, Stewardship Theory, Stakeholders' Theory, and Resource Dependence Theory. We predict that one of these competing corporate governance theories will *replace* or *integrate* with agency theory in the near future. We base our prediction on the fact that agency theory has thus far failed to resolve the conflict of interest between management and shareholders. In this chapter, we give a brief introduction to each theory and cite some examples from academic literature on the appropriateness of these competing theories to resolve the issue of agency costs, which is fundamentally and historically the underlying motivation for corporate governance mechanisms.

AGENCY THEORY

Corporate governance codes are grounded in the agency theory and the need to reduce agency costs. Underlying agency theory is a mismatch between the interests of managers and shareholders; therefore, corporate governance is initiated to resolve this conflict and help reduce agency costs. That is, effective corporate governance is expected to lower monitoring, auditing, and other private costs of investors. In fact, the discussion about the separation of ownership and control which initiated agency theory goes back to Adam Smith's book *The Wealth of Nations* that was first published in 1776. An excerpt from that book states that:

> "The directors of such [joint-stock] companies, however, being the managers rather of other people's money than of their own, it cannot well be expected, that they should watch over it with the same anxious vigilance with which the partners in a private copartnery frequently watch over their own. Like the stewards of a rich man, they are apt to consider attention to small matters as not for their master's honour, and very easily give themselves a dispensation from having it. Negligence and profusion, therefore, must always prevail, more or less, in the management of the affairs of such a company"

Smith referred to the separation of ownership and control (or more precisely the conflict of interest) between shareholders and management in his book. Moreover, Smith was the first author to point out the fact that managers act in their own best interests by maximizing their profits and not as an agent for shareholders. Another excerpt from Adam Smith's book states that:

> ''Being the managers of other people's money [rather than their own] . . . it cannot be expected that they should watch over it with the same anxious vigilance . . ..''

For decades following the publication of Smith's book, there was no well-developed theory to explain the separation of ownership and control. In the beginning of the twentieth century, agency theory started to emerge in the pioneer work of Berle and Means (1932). Since that time, many authors have attempted to define the costs that are associated with the separation of ownership and control in organizations. Those costs are said to range from either missed opportunities by a risk-averse management to management recklessness by excessive risk-taker management (Burton 2000). Anecdotal evidence suggests that the presence of good corporate governance mitigates the asymmetric information or reduces the traditional principal-agency problems between stakeholders and managers. Likewise, poor corporate governance intensifies the information asymmetry between stakeholders and managers and hence increases agency costs. Agency Theory is claimed to be helpful only when contracting incentives fail to mitigate agency costs, are impossible to apply, or are incomplete.

Although there exists widespread recognition of agency theory as the primary theory underlying corporate governance systems, critics have started to aggressively comment on the appropriateness of agency theory in reducing agency costs, especially since the collapse of large, international firms (Enron and others) and more recently, the global financial turmoil that began in late 2007 and early 2008. For example, Hart (1995) criticizes agency theory for dealing with the firm as a 'black box'. Although agency theory predicts that corporate governance will maximize shareholders wealth by strengthen an organization's governance structure, little is known about how this structure translates into profit maximization. Another criticism of agency theory is the lack of feedback. We need to know whether the actual outputs are originated through the traditional inputs we entered into the process. In other words, we need to verify that shareholders' wealth maximization is indeed the output of a well developed governance structure and nothing else. In the presence of an endogenous association between corporate governance structures and firm performance, feedback on the effectiveness of corporate governance systems seems impossible. We also need to be able to take corrective or preventive actions in response to undesired outputs from weak corporate governance structures. Unfortunately, agency theory does not enable us to do so.

In addition to the use of agency theory in prior corporate governance research, we find some studies that employ competing theories, such as Contingency Theory, Stewardship Theory, Stakeholders Theory, and Resource Dependence Theory. The purpose of these competing theories is to increase our understanding of the value of corporate governance to firms. In the following section, we introduce the basic concepts of each of these competing theories. We are not claiming that these are the only competing theories; rather, our discussion tends to the practical side in the sense that we focus on the most cited governance theories that are reported in the academic literature.

Contingency Theory

Contingency theory maintains an *institutional* perspective in viewing the relationship between corporate governance codes and firm value. According to contingency theory, corporate governance mechanisms might positively or negatively affect firm performance *only* after controlling for some moderating variables that would significantly impact the relationship between the proxy used for corporate governance and firm outcomes. For example, some of the moderating variables that would significantly impact the association between financial reporting quality and corporate governance mechanisms is the environment underlying financial reporting quality such as: information uncertainty, business complexity, environmental factors, market conditions (bull or bear market), firm credit risk and the probability of default, country specific factors (recession or expansion), and time factors. Although these are the factors most commonly studied with respect to the success or failure of corporate governance codes, there are other factors that are not as commonly studied. For instance, firm configurations are documented to affect firm value (Ketchen, Combs, Russell, Shook, Dean, Runge, Lohrke, Naumann, Haptonstahl, Baker, Bechstein, Handler, Honig, and Lamoureux 1997). Other possible variables are those associated with the board of directors (e.g., high levels of experience, appropriate team size, moderate levels of variation in age and team tenure) which are discussed in McIntyre, Murphy, and Mitchell (2007).

STEWARDSHIP THEORY

Agency Theory is criticized for ignoring the non-financial, psychological, and sociological aspects associated with executives (Donaldson and Davis, 1991). However, stewardship theory focuses on 'models of man' in which the person is motivated by the need to achieve, the satisfaction gained through successfully doing a challenging job, the recognition from exercising responsibility and achieving power from his work environment. Executives might perceive their future as part of their corporate success and prosperity in the market because corporate success will increase demand on executives of these successful corporations in the job market and might also increase their pension rights. Stewardship theory holds the view that executives need to exercise full power over the firm. Executives need to feel unchallenged by the board of directors.

Moreover, Stewardship theory holds that managers are inherently trustworthy and act for the best interest of shareholders and various stakeholders. For example, it is expected that the CEO who wears many hats by working as the chairman and director at the same time - a phenomena known as 'CEO duality' in the literature - will positively impact firm performance. Stewardship theory is based on the assumption that managers are responsible and inherently trustworthy, that they maximize the firm's profit in order to protect their reputation and maintain their power over management. In this line of thought, executives strive to show their individual performance through achieving high firm profits. Stewardship theory claims that outside directors might have close social ties with the top senior management. By the same token, Lipton and Lorsch (1992) argue that "the norms of behavior in most boardrooms are dysfunctional". The dysfunctionality of independent board of directors stems from the assumption that directors are sometimes following the footsteps of executives without daring to criticize, discuss, or effectively taking the role of 'supervisors' on executives' activities. Donaldson and Davis (1991) provide empirical support for Stewardship Theory. They investigate the effect of CEO duality on shareholders wealth as proxied by returns on equity and gains in shareholders' wealth. They suggest that the CEO duality leads to higher returns for shareholders. They also find that the positive effects of CEO duality are not due to the spurious effects of long-term compensation.

Stakeholder Theory

The claim that agency costs exist only between management and shareholders is indeed restricted. Actually, the conflict exists between the firm and all interested parties involved with the firm such as employees, communities, regulatory agencies, customers, suppliers, government, and political groups. These groups or parties are called the *stakeholders* of the firm who have intrinsic value and whose interests might not be in line with those of the firm. Stakeholder theory describes the nature of the firm, the way managers think about different methods to manage the firm, how board members think about the diverse interests of stakeholders, and how corporations are actually managed. The Stakeholders descriptive approach underlying Stakeholder theory seems crucial to the success of corporate governance codes. Stakeholder theory incorporates governance codes among the organizational constellations to ensure minimizing the conflict of interest among all different interested parties (Donaldson and Preston, 1995). An interesting possibility to reduce agency costs would be to integrate stakeholder theory with agency theory to better explain corporate governance structures.

Resource Dependence Theory

Resource dependence theory argues that the board of directors should provide the resources needed by the firm (Daily, Dalton, and Cannella, 2003). Underlying this theory is the idea that specialized outside members should be members of the board of directors. Such a composition for the board of directors is deemed necessary to fulfill the firm's diverse resource needs (such as legal needs and financial expertise). With a diverse board, firm performance is expected to improve, while the gap (or conflict of interest) between management and shareholders is expected to narrow. We find a stream of literature that supports the resource dependence theory (e.g., Dalton, Daily, Johnson, and Ellstrand, 1999; Hillman, Cannella, and Paetzold, 2000; Johnson, Daily, and Ellstrand, 1996). However, as we noted before, research is heavily focused on the monitoring/controlling role of the board of directors, and underestimates the resource dependence and services roles of the board of directors, which could impact (i.e., reduce) agency costs.

References

Berle, A., and Means, G. 1932. The modern corporation and private property. New York: Macmillan, as cited in Dalton, D. R., Daily, C. M., Certo, S. T., and Roengpitya, R. 2003. Meta-analyses of financial performance and equity: Fusion or confusion? *Academy of Management Journal* 46: 13-26.

Burton, P. 2000. Antecedents and consequences of corporate governance structures. *Corporate Governance* 8: 194-203.

Dalton, D., Daily, C., Johnson, J. , and Ellstrand, A. 1999. Number of directors and financial performance: A Meta-analysis. *The Academy of Management Journal* 42 (6): 674-686.

Daily, C. , Dalton, D., and Cannella, A. 2003. Corporate Governance: Decades of dialogue and data. *Academy of Management Review* 28: 371-382.

Donaldson, L. and Davis, J. 1991. Stewardship theory or agency theory: CEO governance and shareholder returns. *Australian Journal of Management* 16 (1): 49-66.

Donaldson T., and Preston, L. 1995. The stakeholder theory of the corporation: concepts, evidence, and implications. *Academy of Management Review* 20 (1): 65-91.

Hart, O. 1995. Corporate Governance: Some theory and implications. *The Economic Journal* 105 (430): 678-689.

Hillman, A., Cannella, A., Jr., and Paetzold, R. 2000. The resource dependence role of corporate directors: Strategic adaptation of board composition in response to environmental change. *Journal of Management Studies* 37: 235-256.

Johnson, J., Daily, C., and Ellstrand, A. 1996. Boards of directors: A review and research agenda. *Journal of Management* 22: 409-438.

Ketchen, D., Combs, J., Russell, G., Shook, C., Dean, M., Runge, J., Lohrke, F., Naumann, S., Haptonstahl, D., Baker, R., Bechstein, B., Handler, C., Honig, H., and Lamoureux, S. 1997. Organizational configurations and performance: A Meta analysis. *Academy of Management Journal* 40: 223-240.

Lipton, M., and Lorsch, J. 1992. A modest proposal for improved corporate governance. *Business Lawyer* 48 (1): 59- 77.

McIntyre, M., Murphy, S., and Mitchell, P. 2007. The top team: examining board composition and firm performance. *Corporate Governance* 7 (5): 547-561.

Smith, A. 1776. *The Wealth of Nations. Edited* by Edwin Cannan, 1904. Reprint edition 1937. New York, Modern Library.

Chapter 3

SARBANES OXLEY ACT OF 2002 – INTENDED AND UNINTENDED CONSEQUENCES

SARBANES OXLEY ACT 2002

The Public Accounting Reform and Investor Protection Act is commonly referred to as the Sarbanes-Oxley Act of 2002 (hereafter SOX 2002). SOX 2002 was enacted on July 30, 2002 in response to a number of major accounting scandals in the U.S. market such as Enron, Tyco International, and WorldCom. These scandals resulted in a collapse of these companies' share prices and hence significantly impacted investor's confidence in the reliability of publicly-traded companies' financial statements. Therefore, various sections/provisions of SOX 2002 were issued to restore investors' confidence in the reliability and quality of financial statements. Examples of these sections of SOX 2002 that have been issued and widely debated in the accounting, finance, and law literatures are Sections 302, 404, 406, and 407. Section 302 focuses on improving corporate responsibility of financial reports, Section 404 focuses on management's assessment of internal controls, Section 406 mandates the disclosure of corporate codes of ethics, and Section 407 mandates disclosure of financial expertise in the 10-K filling.

SOX 2002 was not initiated as a result of thorough empirical research (Romano, 2005; and Carcello, 2005); however, this lack of research has prompted academics to investigate the provisions of SOX 2002, as well as how these provisions are meeting the objectives intended by Congress. Most of the academic research on SOX 2002 centers on answering these questions: What did SOX 2002 do to firm value? Has SOX 2002 improved or worsened the quality of financial reporting? What are the costs and benefits of SOX 2002 and its subsequent provisions? An important question that has not yet been investigated is: What is the *net benefit* of SOX 2002 to U.S. firms and the U.S. economy? We predict that the answers to these questions cannot be easily captured through a formal investigation using qualitative and quantitative firm-level data. However, we believe that these questions are very important to understand whether firms are reaping any benefits from SOX 2002. That is, do the benefits outweigh the costs? Are there unintended consequences? Answering these questions requires interdisciplinary studies that integrate micro- with macro-economics into one paradigm.

We also note that studies of the implications of SOX 2002 on firm value have been descriptive in nature and tend to describe the circumstances surrounding SOX 2002 in relation to the firm value. Examples of some sections of SOX 2002 that attracted the attention of accounting, finance, auditing, and law researchers are discussed below with an emphasize on the implications of these provisions on firm value. In depth analysis on the various aspects of firm value that are affected by corporate governance best practices, or more specifically SOX 2002 provisions, are discussed later in parts two and three of this book.

SARBANES OXLEY ACT 2002, SECTION 302

Section 302 focuses on improving corporate responsibility for financial reports. It requires management to evaluate the effectiveness of disclosure related to internal controls and procedures. Although the COSO framework broadly defines internal control in terms of achieving (1) the effectiveness and efficiency of operations, (2) reliability of financial reporting, and (3) compliance with applicable laws and regulations (Statements on Auditing Standards, Section 319), Sarbanes-Oxley only pertains to internal control related to the reliability of financial reporting.

SARBANES OXLEY ACT 2002, SECTION 401

The main purpose of Section 401 is to require preparers and issuers of financial statements to prepare and disclose accurate financial statements that do not contain material incorrect information. These financial statements should also include all material off-balance sheet liabilities, obligations, or transactions.

SARBANES OXLEY ACT 2002, SECTION 404

Section 404 requires management of publicly traded firms to evaluate their internal control systems. Additionally, it requires a firm's external auditor to provide an opinion regarding management's assessment of internal controls. Section 404 opinions are important because they provide an *unambiguous* signal from an independent third-party (external auditor) about the effectiveness of a firm's internal control (Ashbaugh-Skaife, Collins, Kinney, and LaFond, 2008). Numerous studies examine firms reporting internal control weaknesses in relation to Section 404. Some of these studies focus on the pros and cons of Section 404 versus Section 302, the determinants of internal control deficiency, and/or the consequences of Section 302 and Section 404 on the auditing profession and the audit committee.

Section 404 is a highly debated yet important provision of SOX 2002. It was named "the section of unintended consequences" because it imposes a burden on, and carries costs and benefits to, the SEC and registrants. Gupta and Nayar (2006) suggest that internal control weaknesses might trigger a debt ratings review and consequently increase borrowing costs (and default risk) in the short run. Ashbaugh-Skaife, Collins, and Kinney (2007) introduce a theoretical model of factors that contribute to internal control deficiency (hereafter ICD) from one side (internal control risk factors) and management's incentives to disclose and report ICD from another side.

Research questions on Section 404 include whether the determinants of ICD *post* Section 404 differ from those *pre* Section 404. Prior to Section 404, ICD disclosure was not mandatory, so managers were making a tradeoff between the expected benefits from the discovery and disclosure of ICDs and the costs associated with disclosing ICDs. However, post Section 404, managers have no discretion in reporting the discoverable ICD – managers are required to disclose and report ICDs. Another research question in this domain is whether the ICDs post Section 404 increased or decreased. This question derived from the question of benefits versus costs of SOX 2002 and whether this legislation contributed to decreasing internal control risk factors, ICDs, and hence increasing the reliability of financial statements. Other questions underlying this stream of research include: Whether the disclosure of ICD resolves market uncertainty, increases/decreases the cost of equity capital, and/or contains value relevant information to market wide-participants, especially investors of firms with ICD.

SARBANES OXLEY ACT 2002, SECTION 406

Section 406 requires public firms to disclose their code of ethics for senior financial officers of the firm, and if there are any waivers granted to these individuals.

SARBANES OXLEY ACT 2002, SECTION 407

Section 407 requires disclosure of audit committee members that the company designates as "financial experts." Section 407 expands the Securities and Exchange Commission proposal that requires only individuals with accounting experience to fulfill the role of financial expertise. Section 407 allows other types of expertise, such as "supervisors" of the financial reporting function (e.g., CEOs) and "users" of financial reports in a professional capacity (e.g., financial analysts and venture capitalists). Section 407 mandates that at least one qualified individual on the audit committee must be designated (i.e., named in the10-K) as a financial expert, otherwise the firm must specify, in the 10-K, reasons why there is no designated financial expert.

SARBANES OXLEY ACT 2002, SECTION 409

Section 409 requires firms to disclose, on a regular basis, information regarding material changes in their financial condition or operations. This disclosure of material changes should be done using supportive qualitative information, graphical representation, and in an easy format to understand by users of financial statements.

Sarbanes Oxley Act 2002, Section 802

Section 802 stipulates penalties in terms of fines and/or up to 20 years imprisonment for any deliberate action by issuers of financial statements that aims at falsifying, altering, canceling, destroying documents or tangible evidence with the intent of influencing a legal investigation. The same provision also imposes fines and/or up to 10 years imprisonment on any accountant who recklessly violates the requirements of maintaining all audit and/or review papers for a period of five years.

Sarbanes Oxley Act 2002, Section 906

Section 906 requires corporate responsibility for financial reports, i.e., a written certification by the Chief Executive Officer and Chief Financial Officer (or their equivalent) that claims the financial statements are in full compliance with SEC regulations and fairly represent the financial condition and results of operations of the firm. Section 906 also imposes penalties of not more than $1,000,000 or up to ten years imprisonment in case the certification provided to the SEC is falsified. A fine of not more than $5,000,000 or up to 20 years imprisonment is also imposed on any officer who willfully certifies any financial statements that are not prepared in accordance with SEC rules and regulations.

The Intended and Unintended Consequences of Sarbanes Oxley Act 2002

Research on the planned and unplanned consequences of SOX 2002 includes investigating the impact and consequences of each issued provision of SOX 2002 on firm outcomes (e.g., firm value, performance, voluntary disclosure) internal control structure (e.g., internal control deficiencies, material restatements, cost of equity and debt) or even firms' interactions with independent third parties (e.g., financial analysts, capital markets, and external auditors). As a result of this extensive body of research, the unplanned consequences of SOX 2002 include both some negative (undesirable) and positive (desirable) implications. We note that most of the research on the unplanned consequences of SOX 2002 provisions is ex-*post*. We argue that this latter observation may be a fruitful point for future research on corporate governance in the sense that "proactive" corporate governance mechanisms are more important than "passive" ones. In this section, we do not attempt to address the question of whether benefits from SOX 2002 exceed its costs; rather, we highlight the effects of SOX 2002 on firms, in general, and further discuss the bright and dark sides of SOX 2002 on firms.

SOX 2002: THE *BRIGHT* SIDE

Based on the academic literature, SOX 2002 has increased board meetings, the percentage of outside directors on the board, and representation of financial expertise on the audit committee. SOX 2002 has also enhanced the transparency of financial reporting, strengthened corporate governance systems, resulted in better business processes and financial statements, and enhanced organizations' enterprise risk management. Krishnan and Ye (2005) find that financial expertise and audit committees offer positive monitoring effects on firms. They document that audit committees are associated with an increased likelihood of seeking ratification from shareholders. SOX 2002 has also made a significant impact on the audit process and profession. DeFond and Francis (2005) claim that the number of audit failures after SOX 2002 has declined and even reached an annual failure rate that approaches zero.

Related, Lobo and Zhou (2006) suggest that SOX 2002 has altered management discretionary behavior and makes it more conservative. They find that managers report lower discretionary accruals after SOX 2002 than in the period preceding SOX 2002. However, the increased conservatism noted by these authors might be due to the increased awareness in the corporate environment, management's fear of litigation risk, and/or other market-wide variables and psychological factors.

Likewise, Krishnan (2005) examines the association between audit committee quality (such as size, independence, expertise) and the quality of corporate internal control (by using a dummy variable for the presence or absence of internal control problems). She uses a sample of 128 firms over the years 1997 through 2000, and the results indicate that an independent audit committee and an audit committee with financial expertise are highly associated with less likelihood of internal control problems. However, the results of Krishnan's (2005) study might underestimate this association since the sample period is pre-SOX 2002. There could have been firms with internal control weaknesses that did not disclose these weaknesses due to lack of law enforcement prior to SOX 2002. Therefore, we find that post-SOX 2002, audit committee quality (both independence and financial expertise) is still an important determinant of a healthy/successful internal control environment as it was pre-SOX 2002.

SOX 2002: THE *DARK* SIDE

On the other side, some of the negative implications of SOX 2002 include conglomerating of unrelated companies, delisting from the U.S. capital markets (one of the international negative impacts of corporate governance to the firm), banning non-audit fees, increasing audit fees as a proxy for audit quality, and altering earnings management approach. That is, managers switched after SOX 2002 from aggressively manipulating earnings using discretionary accruals to using real activities manipulations such as making significant reductions in Research and Development costs or giving extreme sales discounts to boost sales. Moreover, DeFond and Francis (2005) argue that SOX 2002 broke down the auditing profession by increasing audit fees by 50-100 percent, banning non-audit services performed by the incumbent auditor, and changing auditing from a self-regulated industry to an industry that is now regulated by a quasi-governmental agency, which is the Public Company Accounting Oversight Board (PCAOB). In the same domain, Gupta and Nayar (2006) suggest that the disclosure of internal control weaknesses might trigger a debt ratings review and consequently increase the borrowing cost (and default risk) of a firm in the short run. Further, Beneish, Billings, and Hodder (2008) document an increase in audit fees due to the internal control reporting requirements of SOX 2002, based in part on the increase in billable hours of auditors.

Additionally, SOX 2002 creates threats to Small and Medium Sized firms (SMEs), since SMEs rely more on manual controls versus automated controls which would make the cost of compliance with SOX 2002 very high compared to expected benefits of the compliance. Arnold, Benford, Canada, Kuhn, and Sutton (2007) investigate the impact of SOX 2002 on the performance of SMEs and find that SOX 2002 resulted in both costs and benefits to SMEs. SOX 2002 indeed affects the production cycle times, information technology investment, supply chain performance, and market competitiveness. SOX 2002 also resulted in increased de-listings on U.S. exchanges and increased listings on non-U.S. exchanges. This impact can be explained by increased costs embodied with the application of SOX 2002 and the inability of SMEs to maintain competitiveness in the marketplace. SOX 2002 even made some SMEs' management decide to go private, rather than being a public company, in order to survive. Also, the internal control regulations under SOX 2002 are incompatible with many SMEs' needs and consume these companies' resources. SOX 2002 draws the funds away from Research and Development expenses in these SMEs. The internal control regulations also impacted the outsourcing and supply chain related activities because management must assess the internal controls of the partner organization as they relate to activities affecting that company.

Another threat introduced by SOX 2002 is reported in Ashbaugh-Skaife, Collins, Kinney, and LaFond's (2008) study, which investigates the effects of internal control deficiencies and their remediation on accrual quality. This study documents that when auditors confirm remediation of reported internal control deficiencies, accrual quality increases relative to firms that do not remediate their internal control deficiencies. Overall, results suggest that the quality of internal control affects the quality of accruals. Likewise, Ogneva, Subramanyam, and Raghunandan (2007) find that firms with internal control weaknesses post-SOX 2002 have higher implied cost of equity capital.

Beneish, Billings, and Hodder (2008) document a negative stock price reaction to internal control weakness disclosures using a short-window design under both Section 302 and Section 404. They argue that this negative stock price reaction attributes to lowered earnings' expectations and increased cost of equity. However, they document no significant stock price or cost-of-equity effects associated with Section 404 disclosures. Therefore, it is possible that internal control deficiencies could have cost-of-equity implications that are not noticeable in prior research.

Similarly, Hammersley, Myers, and Shakespeare (2008) and Gupta and Nayar (2006) investigate the market reaction to SOX 2002. Hammersley et al. (2008) study the market reaction to disclosure of internal control weaknesses under Section 302 and find that the market negatively reacts to internal control weakness disclosure and this reaction depends on the magnitude of the internal control weakness. Gupta and Nayar's (2006) study examines whether Section 404 conveys value-relevant information to the U.S. equity market. They use the voluntary disclosures made by Securities and Exchange Commission's registrants and find that internal control weakness disclosures provide significant value-relevant information to the capital markets because such disclosures are associated with a negative stock price reaction. This reaction is lessened when management disclosed specific remediation steps taken to correct the reported internal control material weakness. Also, the price reaction is less negative for firms employ a Big-4 auditing firm as their external auditors. This finding suggests that internal control weaknesses might trigger a debt ratings review, increase borrowing cost and default risk in the short run, as well as increase Big-4 involvement in the auditing process.

REFERENCES

Arnold, V., Benford, T., Canada, J., Kuhn, J., and Sutton, S. 2007. The unintended consequences of Sarbanes-Oxley on technology innovation and Supply Chain integration. *Journal of Emerging Technologies in Accounting* 4: 103-121.

Ashbaugh-Skaife, H., Collins, D., and Kinney, W. 2007. The discovery and reporting of internal control deficiencies prior to SOX 2002-mandated audits. *Journal of Accounting and Economics* 44: 166-192.

______ , ______ , ______ , and LaFond, R. 2008. The effect of SOX 2002 internal control deficiencies and their remediation on accrual quality. *The Accounting Review* 83 (1): 217-250.

Beneish, M., Billings, M., and Hodder, L. 2008. Internal control weaknesses and information uncertainty. *The Accounting Review* 83 (3): 665-704

Carcello, J. 2005. Discussion of audit research after Sarbanes-Oxley. *Auditing: A Journal of Practice and Theory* 24: 31-40.

DeFond, M. and Francis, J. 2005. Audit Research after Sarbanes-Oxley. *Auditing: A Journal of Practice and Theory* 24: 5-30.

Denis, D. 2001. Twenty-five years of corporate governance research…and counting. *Review of Financial Economics* 10: 191-212.

Gupta, P. and Nayar, N. 2006. Information content of control deficiency disclosures under the Sarbanes – Oxley Act: An empirical investigation. *International Journal of Disclosure and Governance* 4 (1): 3–23.

Hammersley, J., Myers, L., and Shakespeare, C. 2008. Market reactions to the disclosure of internal control weaknesses and to the characteristics of those weaknesses under Section 302 of the Sarbanes Oxley Act of 2002. *Review of Accounting Studies* 13: 141–65.

Krishnan, J. 2005. Audit committee quality and internal control: An empirical analysis. *The Accounting Review* 80 (2): 649-675.

______ and Ye, Z. 2005. Why some companies seek shareholder ratification on auditor selection. *Accounting Horizons* 19 (4): 237-254.

Lobo, G. and Zhou, J. 2006. Did conservatism in financial reporting increase after the Sarbanes-Oxley Act? Initial Evidence. *Accounting Horizons* 20 (1): 57-73.

Ogneva, M., Subramanyam, K., and Raghunandan, K. 2007. Internal control weakness and cost of equity: Evidence from SOX 2002 Section 404 disclosures. *The Accounting Review* 82 (5): 1255-1297.

Romano, R. 2005. The Sarbanes-Oxley Act and the making of quack corporate governance. *Yale Law Journal* 114: 1521–1611.

Sarbanes-Oxley Act 2002 web page: http://www.soxlaw.com/index.htm

Part II. Corporate Governance and U.S. Firm Performance

Chapter 4

CORPORATE GOVERNANCE AND STOCK PRICE PERFORMANCE

This chapter attempts to answer the question: Does Wall Street appreciate corporate governance? In order to answer this question, we first need to understand the role corporate governance might play in affecting a firm's stock price performance (stock returns). Jensen and Meckling (1976) define the firm as: *"a legal fiction which serves as a nexus for contracting relationships and which is also characterized by the existence of divisible residual claims on the assets and cash-flows of the organization which can generally be sold without the permission of the other contracting individuals"*. Therefore, assessing the impact of corporate governance codes on U.S. firm performance (e.g., stock prices/returns) should be done by observing the change in shareholders' wealth before and after the implementation of a certain governance provision (Denis, 2001). If the shareholders' wealth increased after the issuance of a certain governance provision, assuming that other factors remain constant, then this provision reduces agency costs and helps align the interests of management with those of shareholders, otherwise the governance provision fails to reduce the agency costs. In this chapter, we review empirical evidence on the association between corporate governance and stock price performance in U.S. firms.

ENDOGENOUS GOVERNANCE - PERFORMANCE RELATIONSHIP

While researchers take into account the endogenous governance/ performance association in their research models, little is known regarding why, when and how endogeneity exists in the first place. It is common that firms are more likely to have a new board of directors or increase the number of independent outside directors on the board after mergers and acquisitions or after having a series of poor financial performances. In this latter case, researchers who investigate the association between corporate governance and firm performance might erroneously conclude that corporate governance is associated with poor financial performance and ignore the fact that the poor financial performance of their sample firms urges the need for immediate appointments of outside directors. Hence, poor firm performance might trigger the need for an effective corporate governance structure and not the other way round.

Therefore, to accurately study the association between corporate governance and firm performance, a set of control variables should be included in the regression model to control for the endogenous structure of corporate governance and firm performance. Additionally, various firm performance measures might exhibit differing needs for corporate governance mechanisms and hence one corporate governance measure for all kinds of firm performances would not mitigate agency costs. This latter premise indicates that corporate governance usefulness to the firm is more like a context or a situation-based system which depends on the configurations of organizations and the business environment. Moreover, agency costs are not the same for all firms. They vary due to many factors (Jensen and Meckling, 1976). The factors that affect corporate governance implementation and hence effectiveness include: firm-specific factors related to contracting and monitoring activities, the degree of competition in the managerial labor market, and the market for corporate control. Consequently, it is imperative to control for such firm-specific factors when conducting an experimental or an archival study on the association between corporate governance and firm performance.

How Do Stock Prices Respond to Good versus Bad Corporate Governance Structure?

Stock market forces, such as market competition and market share prices, discipline management by imposing higher cost of capital on low performing firms. A firm's stock price also synchronizes with the firm's performance. When a firm discloses its financial statements, high performing firms are usually rewarded by the market with increases in their stock price. Likewise, low performing firms typically experience a decrease in their stock prices. This stock price – firm performance relationship can be explained by the fact that the disclosure of high performing firms are perceived in the market as *good* news while the disclosure of low performing firms are rated by market participants as *bad* news and hence in the latter case, a drop in stock prices is expected. Such a drop in stock prices is a signal to poor management and a type of punishment for substandard firm performance. The intervening impact of effective corporate governance codes on the relationship between stock prices and firm performance comes from the fact that good governance codes enhance the transparency, accuracy, and credibility of financial statements disclosed to various market-wide participants. Therefore, it is expected that the market will typically reward firms with strong corporate governance systems in terms of higher stock prices.

Corporate Governance and Stock Prices/Returns

In this section, we review empirical results on the association between corporate governance and stock price performance in U.S. firms. The theoretical concept suggests that higher stock prices/returns will obtain in the presence of strong corporate governance structure. However, the empirical evidence we find on the association between the strength of corporate governance and stock prices/returns are contradictory and inconclusive to support the theoretical basis underlying such claimed association. Possible explanations for these mixed results are discussed in this chapter.

Gompers, Ishii, and Metrick (2003) were among the lead researchers to empirically investigate the relationship between corporate governance and stock price performance. They construct a "governance index or G-Index" using 24 distinct corporate governance provisions to proxy for the level of shareholder rights at 1500 firms from September 1990 to December 1999.

Firms in the highest deciles of the index were in the "Dictatorship Portfolio" and referred to as having the highest management power/weakest shareholder rights. Firms in the lowest deciles of the index were called the "Democracy Portfolio" and were characterized as having the lowest management power/strongest shareholder rights. The results of Gompers's et al. (2003) indicate that the Democracy Portfolio outperforms the Dictatorship Portfolio by 8.5 percent per year. In other words, an investment strategy that purchased shares in the Democracy Portfolio and sold shares in the Dictatorship Portfolio earned abnormal returns of 8.5 percent per year. Gompers et al. (2003) find that firms with stronger shareholder rights (or stronger corporate governance structure) had higher firm value, higher profits, higher sales growth, lower capital expenditures, and made fewer corporate acquisitions. They also find evidence that firms with weak shareholder rights (or weaker corporate governance structure) were less profitable and had lower growth than other firms in their industry. Gompers et al. (2003) explain their results by arguing that weak shareholder rights (or weak corporate governance structure) cause additional agency costs. Also, weak shareholder rights might cause investors to lower their expectations about the firms' future cash flows, which results in lower stock prices. Gompers et al. (2003) further interpret their results by using two competing explanations. Either poor corporate governance causes agency costs, or the abnormal returns resulted from their study are due to some unobservable firm characteristics that are correlated with the G-Index they constructed.

Consequently, Core, Guay, and Rusticus (2006) extend the study made by Gompers et al. (2003) by attempting to distinguish between the two competing explanations offered by Gompers et al.'s (2003) study. The second explanation provided by Gompers et al. (2003) maintains that corporate governance variables or the G-Index did not cause the abnormal stock returns observed in their study. Thus, other factors might exist that are highly associated with the G-Index (or governance variables used to calculate the G-Index) and hence other non-governance variables caused the documented abnormal stock returns during the sample period.

Core et al. (2006) test for the association between corporate governance and operating performance, and find that the G-index had a significant negative association with future operating performance. This result supports Gompers et al.'s (2003) results, suggesting that firms with higher G-indices have greater agency costs. Core et al. (2006) also find that takeover frequencies of weak governance firms increased over the 1990s and weak governance firms were taken over at about the same rate as were strong governance firms. Overall, Core et al. (2006) find no causal relationship between corporate governance and stock returns, contrary to what had been documented by Gompers et al. (2003) study. Core et al. (2006) check the robustness of their results by testing whether the abnormal stock returns resulted from time-period-specific irregularity that is correlated with governance, and the results confirmed their first conclusion regarding no relationship between corporate governance and stock returns. Also contrary to Gompers's et al. (2003) finding of no significant relationship between shareholders rights and operating performance, Core et al. (2006) find evidence that weak shareholder rights are associated with lower operating performance. Thus, Core et al. (2006) conclude that a relationship exists between shareholder rights and operating performance but no relationship exists between corporate governance and stock returns.

In the same vein, Johnson, Moorman, and Sorescu (2009) examine whether the long-term abnormal return results documented by Gompers et al. (2003) are driven by non-governance factors. Following Gompers et al. (2003), Johnson et al. (2009) classify firms with a governance index of 5 or less as *Democracies*, and firms with a governance index of 14 variables or more as *Dictatorships*. For each Democracy firm, they selected a control firm (pseudo-Democracies) that was *not* a Democracy firm with similar industry characteristics. They find that the abnormal returns of Democracy firms over the 1990s were almost identical to those of pseudo-Democracy firms, and the abnormal returns of Dictatorship firms were almost identical to those of pseudo-Dictatorship firms. Results indicate that neither Democracies nor Dictatorships (firms with strong versus weak corporate governance structures) earn statistically significant abnormal returns over the 1990s. These results are consistent with an efficient capital markets view in which investors properly value and price shareholder rights. Johnson et al.'s (2009) results imply that good governance positively affects firm value and that investors recognize and impound that value into share prices quickly and accurately. Johnson et al. (2009) also find significant positive abnormal returns of approximately 8.5 percent per year on a hedge portfolio that takes long positions in Democracy firms and short positions in Dictatorships based on the same sample used in Gompers et al. (2003).

In line with the same theme underlying the study made by Gompers et al. (2003), Bebchuk, Cohen, Ferrell (2009) investigate which provisions, among a set of 24 governance provisions, followed by the Investor Responsibility Research Center (IRRC), are associated with firm value and stockholder returns. This study contributes to our understanding on the relationship between corporate governance and firm value and provides a basis for future work. The period under investigation in this study was 1990-2003. Bebchuk et al. (2009) construct a governance index based on four "constitutional" provisions that prevent a majority of shareholders from having their way (i.e., staggered boards, limits to shareholder bylaw amendments, supermajority requirements for mergers, and supermajority requirements for charter amendments), and two "takeover readiness" provisions that boards put in place to be ready for a hostile takeover (poison pills and golden parachutes). Bebchuk, Cohen, Ferrell (2009) find that an increase in the level of the governance index is associated with economically significant reductions in firm valuation, as measured by Tobin's Q.

Relatedly, DeFond, Hann, and Hu, (2005) investigate the effect of audit committee independence (as a corporate governance tool) on stock returns pre-SOX 2002. They use 702 firms with newly appointed outside directors assigned to audit committees, and three-day cumulative abnormal returns as the returns window around the announcement of those newly appointed outside directors. These authors test the market reaction to the appointment of outside directors with financial expertise on the audit committee to study the effect of SOX 2002 on the stock market. They find a positive market reaction to the appointment of outside directors with financial experts assigned on the audit committees. Moreover, this reaction was stronger for firms with strong corporate governance structures. As a result, they conclude that financial expertise on the audit committee helps enhance shareholder value. Likewise, Arbogast, and Thornton (2006) investigate the effect of the SOX 2002 on earnings per share for 500 companies before (2002/2003) and after (2004/2005) the implementation of SOX 2002. As we discussed in Part One of the book, the U.S. Congress passed SOX act in 2002 to enhance the credibility of financial statements and regain public confidence. However, the perception was that SOX 2002 would inhibit profitability because of compliance costs. However, Arbogast, and Thornton (2006) provide evidence to support a positive effect of SOX 2002 on earnings per share.

Interestingly, Cheng (2008) examines the association between board size (as a measure of corporate governance) and firm performance *variability*. Firm performance is measured by a number of proxies such as stock returns, return on assets, Tobin's Q, accounting accruals, extraordinary items, analyst forecast errors, research and development spending/level, and the frequency of acquisition and restructuring activities. Cheng (2008) finds that when board size increases by one standard deviation, the standard deviation of monthly stock returns decreases by 7percent from the mean and 8percent from the median. Overall, results suggest that large board sizes are making less extreme decisions and end up with less variability in corporate performance measures.

Rubach and Picou (2005) examine the reaction of stock prices to the enactment of corporate governance guidelines using an event study methodology on a sample of 141 firms from January 1, 1994 until December 31, 2000. Although the authors expected that the enactment of corporate governance guidelines would increase shareholders value, results reveal that only a few firms had a significant reaction to governance enactment; that is, overall results were not significant. The implications of this study suggest that SEC filings of governance mechanisms are not a strong signal to the market. The results also suggest that the value of governance policies and guidelines are not clear to investors or could result in heterogeneity in investors' beliefs. Hence, the authors recommend that management increase the transparency of their corporate governance guidelines through public disclosure.

In an attempt to define the characteristics of firms with good corporate governance, Khairi, Karaa, and Omri (2007) develop a governance efficiency score (governance index), based on codes of best practices, using a sample of 320 U.S.-listed firms from 1994-2001. The purpose of the study was to establish a benchmarking tool to identify efficient firms that have the best practices and best governance characteristics. Results suggest two groups of firms with opposite governance systems: (1) a non-performing system, characterized by managerial discretion, an ownership concentration, a dominance of the board by the CEO and manager entrenchment; and (2) a high-performing system, characterized by an inside control efficiency and an inside financial control efficiency.

We also find examples of empirical research, based on real world data, that concludes corporate governance is not always directly associated with firm performance (e.g., stock price). This result could be interpreted as follows. First, corporate governance mechanisms may simply not be associated with firm performance. Second, the underlying governance mechanisms might be interacting with some firm performance measures that give rise to invalid conclusions on the association between corporate governance and firm performance. Third, the various organizational structures and configurations might call for various governance structures and codes in the sense that a one-size governance code may not fit all organizations. For example, the production cycle has changed dramatically over the last 25 years from being machine-intensive to being knowledge-intensive (Denis, 2001). Accordingly, governing a business that is machine-intensive is significantly different than governing a business that relies on human knowledge and intelligence.

In sum, the question of whether strong corporate governance leads to higher stock returns is a topic of great interest to corporate governance researchers. While these researchers have tried to answer this question in a variety of contexts with different samples, the results of these studies have been mixed. While several studies cited earlier in this review document the development of a governance score or index, none of these measures have been adopted as the standard for research in this area. Should investors use board governance metrics such as Institutional Shareholder Services (ISS) or Governance Metrics International (GMI) to decide the effectiveness of a company's board? Koehn and Ueng (2005) examine this issue using a sample of 106 US large-cap companies with publicly disclosed ISS ratings for the years 2002 and 2003. Results show a significant negative relation between the governance scores and the annual stock appreciation. Overall, findings suggest no correlation between a high governance score and high quality earnings. The results of Koehn and Ueng's (2005) study did not yield a strong positive correlation between a high governance score and high quality of earnings indicating that investors should not rely on published governance scores by governance metrics firms. Accordingly, more research on those published governance scores (with respect to earnings quality) is needed, or perhaps development of a new metric that is more predictive, would be a valuable endeavor. Therefore, these metrics may not be good indicators of a company's performance or even its board's effectiveness. That is, investors who want to use governance data in their investment decisions should consult multiple data sources, using both quantitative and qualitative information. Consequently, we recommend another potentially useful area for future research which is the area of corporate governance indices.

Additionally, future research could compare and contrast the various measures of "strong" corporate governance versus "weak" corporate governance in an attempt to determine which one might have the strongest psychometric properties (i.e., internal consistency and validity). Such a study might lead to an accepted measure that might bring consensus in results on the association between corporate governance codes and stock price performance. Also, controlling for endogenous governance/performance and conducting further research on its antecedents, characteristics, and consequences on the governance/performance relationship is crucial in enhancing the governance/ performance model and increasing our understanding of the nature and association between corporate governance and firm performance.

Table 1. Corporate Governance and Stock Price Performance

Study	Sample	Corporate Governance Measures	Control Variables	Firm Value Measures	Findings
Bebchuk, Cohen, and Ferrell (2009)	1400-1800 firms: 1990-2003	Entrenchment index based on 24 governance provisions issued by IRRC	Assets, age of firm, whether the firm is incorporated in Delaware, level of insider ownership, ROA, capital expenditures on assets, R & D, and leverage	Tobin's Q	Entrenchment provisions cause lower firm valuation
Johnson, Moorman, and Sorescu (2009)	1000 firms: 1990-1998	Governance index of 14 variables	Control firms matched on industry, size, book-to-market, and momentum.	Abnormal Returns	Overall, good governance positively affects firm value; investors recognize and impound that value into share prices quickly and accurately
Cheng (2008)	1252 firms: 1996-2004	Board size	Board composition, CEO power, accounting profitability, firm size (natural log of assets), growth opportunities (capital expenditures over sales), financial leverage (total debt over assets), diversification (number of business segments), and CEO ownership	Returns, ROA, Tobin's Q, accounting accruals, extraordinary items, analyst forecast errors, R & D spending and level, and the frequency of acquisition and restructuring activities	Large board sizes are making less extreme decisions and end up with less variability in corporate performance measures
Arbogast and Thornton (2006)	47 firms: pre-SOX 2002 (2002/2003) and post-SOX 2002 2004/2005	The event of implementing SOX 2002	None	The mean earnings per share before and after implementation of SOX 2002	A positive effect of SOX 2002 on EPS

Table 1. Corporate Governance and Stock Price Performance (cont.)

Study	Sample	Corporate Governance Measures	Control Variables	Firm Value Measures	Findings
Core, Guay, and Rusticus (2006)	9917 firm-years: 1990-1998	G-index employed by Gompers et al. (2003), shareholder rights	Book-to-market equity and firm size, measured as logarithm of market value of equity	Operating performance and stock returns	G-index had a significant negative association with future operating performance; a relationship exists between shareholder rights and operating performance but no relationship exists between corporate governance and stock returns
Defond, Hann and Hu (2005)	509 firms: 1993-2002	Audit committee independence and financial expertise	Firm size and market-to-book, growth opportunities and leverage	Stock returns	A positive market reaction to the appointment of outside directors with financial experts assigned on audit committees; this reaction was stronger for firms with strong corporate governance structure; financial expertise on audit committee helps enhance shareholder value
Rubach and Picou (2005)	141 firms: 1-1-1994 to 12-31-2000	After enactment of corporate governance guidelines	An event study methodology was used to isolate effect on interest	Stock prices	The value of governance policies and guidelines are not clear to investors
Gompers, Ishii, and Metrick (2003)	1500 firms: 1990-1998	G-Index using 24 distinct corporate governance provisions	The log book-to-market ratio (BM)	Stock returns	Firms with stronger shareholder rights (or stronger corporate governance structure) had higher firm value, higher profits, higher sales growth, lower capital expenditures, and made fewer corporate acquisitions

REFERENCES

Arbogast, G. and Thornton, B. 2006. Strange bedfellows: SOX 2002 and corporate profitability. *The Business Review* 6 (1): 56-61.

Bebchuk, L., Cohen, A., and Ferrell, A. 2009. What Matters in Corporate Governance? *The Review of Financial Studies* 22 (2): 783-827.

Cheng, S. 2008. Board size and the variability of corporate performance. *Journal of Financial Economics* 87: 157-176.

Core, J. , Guay, W., and Rusticus, T. 2006. Does weak governance cause weak stock returns? An examination of firm operating performance and investors' expectations. *The Journal of Finance* 61 (2): 655–687.

DeFond, M., Hann, R., and Hu, X. 2005. Does the market value financial expertise on audit committees of boards of directors? *Journal of Accounting Research* 43: 153-193.

Denis, D. 2001. Twenty-five years of corporate governance research…and counting. *Review of Financial Economics* 10: 191-212.

Gompers, P., Ishii, J., and Metrick, A. 2003. Corporate governance and equity prices. *Quarterly Journal of Economics* 118 (1): 107-155.

Jensen, M. and Meckling, W. 1976. Theory of the firm: managerial behavior, agency costs and ownership structure. *Journal of Financial Economics* 3: 305–360.

Johnson, S., Moorman, T., and Sorescu, S. 2009. A reexamination of corporate governance and equity prices. *The Review of Financial Studies* 22 (11): 4753-4786.

Khiari, W., Karaa, A., and Omri, A. 2007. Corporate governance efficiency: An indexing approach using the stochastic frontier analysis. *Corporate Governance* 7 (2): 148-161.

Koehn, D. and Ueng, J. 2005. Evaluating the evaluators: Should investors trust corporate governance metrics ratings? *Journal of Management and Governance* 9: 111–128.

Rubach, M. and Picou, A. 2005. The enactment of corporate governance guidelines: An empirical examination. *Corporate Governance* 5 (5): 30-38.

Chapter 5

CORPORATE GOVERNANCE AND FIRM OPERATING PERFORMANCE

This chapter reviews empirical evidence regarding the usefulness of corporate governance to U.S. firm operating performance. Most of this literature uses either return on assets or Tobin's Q as measures of a firm's operating performance. We note that the main focus of this body of research is on such variables as characteristics of the board of directors, composition of the board, size of the board, CEO duality, and fees. Hence, we classify the literature on corporate governance and firm operating performance into three sections: board of directors' composition and firm performance, CEO duality and firm performance, and other governance structures and firm performance. We then discuss the extant research for these three sections.

BOARD OF DIRECTORS' COMPOSITION AND FIRM OPERATING PERFORMANCE

Boards of directors can be composed of either insider directors or independent outside directors. Insider directors include officers from inside the company, affiliated outside directors or grey directors who are former officers of the company, or persons who have business with the company (such as investment banks). Independent directors are persons who have no affiliation with the company. Today, almost all U.S. firms have a majority of board members who are independent and outside directors (Bhagat and Black, 2001.) Nevertheless, the extant research on the relationship between board independency/composition and firm performance do not provide conclusive evidence on the usefulness of board independence to firm operating performance.

For example, Bebchuk and Cohen (2005) examine the association between staggered boards and U.S. firms' operating performances as measured by Tobin's Q during the period 1995-2002. Staggered boards is a situation where boards are protected from removal in a hostile takeover. As a result, staggered boards are indications of a weak corporate governance structure. Bebchuk and Cohen (2005) find that staggered boards are causing, and not just reflecting, a significant reduction in Tobin's Q. This result suggests an economically meaningful and positive, significant association between the strength of corporate governance structure and U.S. firm operating performance.

Hillman and Dalziel (2003) contend that boards of directors are responsible for two main functions: a monitoring function and a resource function (bringing resources to the firm). More specifically, boards are responsible for providing advice and counseling, maintaining the legitimacy of business operations, providing channels for communicating information between external organizations and the firm, and showing preferential access to commitments regarding important events that occur outside the firm but might impact the firm. Haniffa and Hudiab (2006) find a significant association between board size and top five substantial shareholdings and both market (Tobin's Q) and accounting (ROA) performance measures. Related, Kiel and Nicholson (2003) find a positive association between board size and firm value, after controlling for firm size. They also find a positive association between insider directors and market based measures of firm performance.

Similarly, Bhagat and Black (2001) examine the relationship between board composition and firm performance. They suspect the validity of the notion that greater board independency "supermajority-independent boards" is associated with greater firm performance. They suggest that firms maintain a moderate number of insider directors on the board (three to five members on a board size of eleven members). Bhagat and Black (2001) find a negative association between board independence and firm performance, and note that the independent directors in their study own a low percentage of their companies' shares. These researchers speculate that the most important criteria is the need for accountability, rather than independence, of directors. Also, some independent directors are not independent enough; they may be indirectly associated with the company. Likewise, some independent directors are simply not on the appropriate corporate committees. Bhagat and Black (2001) further investigate whether the change of the degree of board independence is associated with firm profitability or growth rate in either the contemporaneous or lagged periods. They find no such association. Further, Ezzamel and Watson (1997) find that the presence of outside directors on the board had little impact on profitability.

Finally, Zahra and Pearce (1989) argue that boards of directors are an important aspect of corporate governance due to their critical role in both monitoring managerial actions and formulating a firm's strategic plan. These authors analyze the literature on the effect of boards of directors on corporate financial performance. In light of their review and analysis, the authors suggest a framework for future research that is based on the integration of the four board attributes (composition, characteristics, structure, and process) and three board roles (service, strategy, and control). Finegold, Benson, and Hecht (2007) extend the study made by Zahra and Pearce (1989) by reviewing 105 published studies between 1989 and 2005 on the extent to which corporate boards and firm performance support corporate governance codes. Among the corporate governance codes they test are SOX 2002, and regulations issued by NYSE and NASDAQ. They also test CEO duality and board structure (insider/outsider ratio, size and stability, board ownership, director rewards). Overall, Finegold et al. (2007) find little evidence to suggest specific best practices for boards of directors that would lead to effective firm performance.

Again, results on the usefulness of the composition of the board of directors, as it relates to firm performance, are mixed. Accordingly, due to this lack of consensus regarding the composition of the board (by majority of independent, outsider directors), we are inclined to believe that this aspect is not a key element to high firm performance.

CEO Duality and Firm Operating Performance

CEO duality means that the CEO of a firm also serves as the Chairman of the board of directors. Stated differently, CEO duality is a situation where the CEO chairs the group that is responsible for firm oversight, as well as for monitoring the CEO's performance (Judge, Naoumova, and Koutzevol, 2003). According to agency theory, there is a conflict of interest between the CEO and the Chairman of the board of directors. The CEO should be responsible for *decision management* and the board should monitor *decision control* and align the different interests of shareholders and top management. Anecdotal evidence suggests that if the CEO and the Chairman are separated and the chairman is an outside independent director, the Chairman will have the maximum autonomy he/she needs to achieve the appropriate level of monitoring over the top management and CEO.

On the other hand, according to stewardship theory, management is inherently trustworthy and hence the duality of CEO and Chairman helps the CEO to be a good steward of corporate assets. Stewardship Theory argues that an outside independent Chairman may act naively, due to his/her unfamiliarity with the business environment. Thus, the benefit of separating the CEO and the Chairman disappears. We find inconclusive results supporting or opposing the CEO duality. We find that the two competing theories underpinning CEO duality (Stewardship and Agency theories) stand strongly in opposition to each other. Therefore, future research is needed to resolve this inconclusive result.

Boyd (1995) investigates the relationship between CEO duality and firm performance for a sample of 192 firms. Boyd firstly hypothesizes that duality is negatively associated with performance, yet finds that the duality – performance relationship is moderated by environmental uncertainty. In other words, duality may be negatively associated with firm performance in some situations and positively associated in others. Likewise, Filatotchev, Lien, and Piesse (2005) find that the independence of the Chairman does not affect performance. In the same vein, Heracleous (2001) finds no significant association between CEO duality and board composition (insider/outsider) and corporate performance. He offers four possible explanations for these results: (1) the governance variables nominated as best practices are irrelevant to firm performance; (2) low validity of the operationalization of the governance construct in the study; (3) ignorance of relevant moderating variables in the model; and (4) differences in organizations that require different practices of corporate governance. Stated differently, different types of organizations might require different board practices.

CEO Compensation and Firm Operating Performance

Research on the association between managerial compensation and firm operating performance focuses on two main areas: the level of pay and the sensitivity of the level of pay to managerial performance. In 1992, the SEC issued the Executive Compensation Disclosure Rules that require publicly listed firms to disclose their compensation packages for the top five highly paid executives in the firm. Moreover, the SEC mandates the disclosure of a comparative graph indicating their firm's executive compensation compared to their industry, the executive stock options granted, and the criteria for evaluating their executives' performance. This regulation has moved executive's attention to stock-based compensation plans, and hence, helped in aligning the incentives of managers and executives with those of their shareholders. For example, CEO compensation (incentive alignment) is one of the financial incentives to align the interests of management with those of shareholders. Hence, Core, Holthausen, and Larcker (1999) investigate whether the level of CEO compensation was associated with the quality of firms' corporate governance and whether there was a negative association between governance structure and future performance. The authors used a sample of 495 observations for 205 publicly traded U.S. firms over the years 1982-1984. The results indicate a significant association between board-of-director characteristics and ownership structure (governance measures) and the level of CEO compensation after controlling for economic determinants of the level of CEO compensation. Moreover, CEO compensation was higher when (1) the CEO was also the board chair, (2) the board was larger, (3) the board was mostly composed of outside directors, and (4) the outside directors were appointed by the CEO. Vance (1983) highlights the importance of having independent board committees in monitoring the activities of management and reducing agency costs. He specifically focuses on four board committees: compensation committees, audit committees, nominating committees, and executive committees. Compensating/remunerating committees are responsible for setting the rewards of executive management and the assumption is that these committees help reduce agency costs by restraining management from awarding themselves excessively.

Other Governance Structures and Firm Operating Performance

Other governance structures may be used to reduce agency costs, such as the presence of some independent committees of the board of directors, such as: nominating committees, compensating committees, audit committees, and others. For example, Wier, Laing, and McKnight (2003) analyze the impact of audit committees on firm performance and find that neither the independence nor the quality of the committee membership has a positive effect on firm performance. Another stream of research focuses on analyzing the overall quality of corporate governance through building governance indexes, such as the studies made by: Bauer, Gunster, and Otten (2004); Bebchuk, Cohen, and Ferrell (2009); and Gompers et al. (2003). These authors establish a governance index for their sample of firms and divided the sample into either good or bad governance portfolio. They find an association between corporate governance and firm value. Likewise, Bebchuk, Cohen, and Ferrell (2009) analyze the association between 24 governance measures (provided by the Investor Responsibility Research Center), firm value, and stockholder returns. They find that higher governance measures are associated with higher firm valuation, as measured by Tobin’s Q.

Yermack (1996) examines the association between board size and firm performance as measured by Tobin’s Q using 452 U.S. industrial firms from 1984 to 1991. He finds that firms with smaller board size perform better than their counterparts with larger board size. He also finds that firms with smaller boards show better firm financial rations in general after controlling for company size, industry membership, inside stock ownership, growth opportunities, and alternative corporate governance structure. Likewise, Coles, Daniel and Naveen (2008) suggest that the relationship between board size and firm performance as measured by Tobin’s Q is U shape. In other words, very small or very large board size appears to maximize firm value. However, Coles et al. (2008) demonstrate that firm complexity, research and development intensity, and the number of outside directors on the board moderate the relationship between firm value and board size. Hence, these variables should be controlled while testing the governance-performance relationship. In this vein, Perry and Shivdasani (2005) suggest that acquisition and restructuring are important determinants to consider while investigating the association between corporate governance and firm performance. Perry and Shivdasani (2005) investigate the association between board composition and how likely firms with low performance can recover in response to board composition. They find that firms with a majority of independent, outside directors perform considerably better than those with insider directors.

The results of the literature we reviewed in this chapter suggest that a firm's operating performance may or may not be positively impacted by certain corporate governance mechanisms. For example, firms with better corporate governance have been shown to be highly correlated with better operating performance, higher firm value, higher stock returns, and higher market valuation. In light of the research reported in this section, a number of possible areas seem useful for future research. One such possibility is a study

Table 2. Corporate Governance and Firm Operating Performance

Study	Sample	Corporate Governance Measures	Control Variables	Firm ValueMeasures	Findings
Coles, Daniel and Naveen (2008)	8165 firm years: 1992-2001	Board size	Firm complexity, R & D intensity, number of outside directors on board	Tobin's Q	Relationship between board size and firm performance is U shaped
Finegold, Benson, and Hecht (2007)	Survey of 105 studies: 1985-2005	CEO duality, board structure (insider/outsider ratio, size and stability, board ownership, director rewards)	None	Corporate financial performance	Little evidence on best board practices that would lead to effective firm performance
Khairi, Karaa, and Omri (2007)	320 US-listed firms: 1994-2001	Governance index	Firm size, leverage, divided yield, return on equity	Firm performance as measured by Tobin's Q, best governance characteristics	Two groups of firms: (1) a non-performing system, characterized by managerial discretion, ownership concentration, dominance of board by CEO and manager entrenchment; (2) a high-performing system, characterized by inside control, financial efficiency
Haniffa and Hudiab (2006)	347 firms: 1996-2000	Board size, top five substantial shareholdings	Company size, industry membership, growth opportunities	Market (Tobin's Q) and accounting performance (ROA) measures	A significant association between board size, top five substantial shareholdings, and both market and accounting performance
Bebchuk and Cohen (2005)	IRRC: 1995-2002	Staggered boards	Assets of firm, age of firm, whether the firm is incorporated in DE, dummies for two digit SIC codes, year fixed effects	Tobin's Q	Staggered boards cause, not just reflect, a significant reduction in Tobin's Q. This result suggests economic meaningful and positive significant association between strength of corporate governance structure and US firm operating performance

Table 2. Corporate Governance and Firm Operating Performance (cont.)

Study	Sample	Corporate Governance Measures	Control Variables	Firm Value Measures	Findings
Perry and Shivdasani (2005)	94 firms: 1992-1996	Board composition	Firm size, leverage, ownership structure	Low performance firms as measured by assets, restructuring, or employee layoffs	Firms with majority of independent outside directors perform twice as well as those with inside directors
Bauer Gunster and Otten (2004)	249-269 firms: 2000-2001	Two portfolios of poor versus well-governed firms	Firm's book value of assets, firm age, ROE in current and previous year	Net-Profit-Margin (NPM), Return-on-Equity (ROE), Tobin's Q and stock returns	No association between governance standards and firm performance measures
Bebchuk, Cohen, and Ferrell (2004)	1400-1800 firms: 1990-2003	Entrenchment index based on 24 governance provisions issued by IRRC	Assets, age of firm, whether firm is incorporated in DE, level of insider ownership, ROA, capital expenditures on assets, R & D, leverage	Tobin's Q	Entrenchment provisions cause lower firm valuation
Kiel and Nicholson (2003)	348 firms: 1996	Board size, insider/outsider directors, diversification of firms, number of interlocks	Firm size (total assets, revenues, market capitalization)	Tobin's Q, ROA	A positive association between board size and firm value, after controlling for firm size; positive association between insider directors and market based measures of firm performance
Wier, Laing, and McKnight (2003)	312 firms: 1996	Board structure, audit committee structure, take-over intensity by sector	Sales, leverage ratio, net capital expenditures to total assets	Tobin's Q	No evidence on efficiency of internal corporate governance control; no link between quality of director and firm performance

Table 2. Corporate Governance and Firm Operating Performance (cont.)

Study	Sample	Corporate Governance Measures	Control Variables	Firm Value Measures	Findings
Heracleous (2001)	Survey of available research	CEO duality and board composition (insider/outsider)	None	Corporate performance	No statistically significant association between CEO duality and board composition (insider/outsider) and corporate performance
Bhagat and Black (2001)	205 firms: 1988-1991 & 1985-1987	Board independence	Industry, board size, firm size	Profitability (Tobin's Q, ROA, assets turnover ratio, operating margin, sales, stock prices) Growth (assets, sales, operating income, cash flow)	No statistically significant association
Core, Holthausen, and Larcker (1999)	205 firms: 1982-1984	CEO compensation (total compensation, cash compensation, salary compensation), Board characteristics (CEO duality and board size) Ownership structure	Firm sales, market-to-book ratio, industry indicators, firm risk, Economic determinants of pay(firm's demand for a high-quality CEO, contemporaneous firm performance, firm risk)	Firm performance (ROA, stock returns)	Strong corporate governance reduces agency costs and increases firm performance; CEO at firms with strong corporate governance receives lower compensation relative to CEO at firms with weak corporate governance
Yermack (1996)	452 US industrial firms: 1984-1991	Board size	Company size, industry membership, inside stock ownership, growth opportunities, alternative corporate governance structure	Tobin's Q	Firms with small boards perform better than counterparts with large board size

Table 2. Corporate Governance and Firm Operating Performance (cont.)

Study	Sample	Corporate Governance Measures	Control Variables	Firm Value Measures	Findings
Boyd (1995)	192 firms: 1980	CEO duality	Environmental factors (munificence, dynamism, complexity)	ROI	Positive under conditions of resource scarcity or high complexity (low munificence environments and high complexity)
Zahra and Pearce (1989)	Survey of available research	Boards of directors	None	Corporate financial performance	Board of directors are weakest tool of corporate governance

of the effect of voluntary versus mandatory governance mechanisms to determine the differential impact each set of mechanisms might have on firm value. In addition, more research on the optimal composition (and characteristics) of board members and audit committee members might be a fruitful area of study. Another interesting topic to pursue might be an examination of the effect of firm-level versus country-level corporate ethics codes (as a form of governance) on firm value (both inter-country and intra-country).

REFERENCES

Bauer, R., Gunster, N., and Otten, R. 2004. Empirical evidence on corporate governance in Europe: The effect on stock returns, firm value and performance. *Journal of Asset Management* 5: 91–104.

Bebchuk, L., Cohen, A., and Ferrell, A. 2009. What Matters in Corporate Governance? *The Review of Financial Studies* 22 (2): 783-827.

Bebchuk, L. and Cohen, A. 2005. The costs of entrenched boards. *Journal of Financial Economics* 78: 409-433.

Bhagat, S. and Black, B. 2001.The non-correlation between board independence and long term firm performance. *Journal of Corporation Law* 27: 231-274.

Boyd, B. 1995. CEO duality and firm performance: A contingency model. *Strategic Management Journal* 16: 301-312.

Coles, J., Daniel, V., and Naveen, L. 2008. Boards: Does one size fit all? *Journal of Financial Economics* 87 (2): 329-356.

Core, J., Holthausen, R., and Larcker, D. 1999. Corporate Governance, Chief Executive Officer Compensation, and Firm Performance. *Journal of Financial Economics* 51: 371-406.

Ezzamel, M. and Watson, R., 1997. Wearing two hats: The conflicting control and management role of nonexecutive directors. In: Keasey, F. et al. (Eds.), Corporate Governance, Economic, Management and Financial Issues. Oxford University Press.

Filatotchev, I., Lien, Y., and Piesse, J. 2005. Corporate Governance and Performance in Publicly Listed, Family-Controlled Firms: Evidence from Taiwan. *Asia Pacific Journal of Management* 22: 257–283.

Finegold, D., Benson, G., and Hecht, D. 2007. Corporate boards and company performance: review of research in light of recent reforms. *Corporate Boards and Company Performance* 15 (5): 865-878.

Gompers, P., Ishii, J., and Metrick, A. 2003. Corporate governance and equity prices. *Quarterly Journal of Economics* 118 (1): 107-155.

Haniffa, R.. and Hudiab, M. 2006. Corporate governance structure and performance of Malaysian listed companies. *Journal of Business Finance and Accounting* 33 (7&8): 1034-1062.

Heracleous, L. 2001. What is the impact of corporate governance on organisational performance? *Corporate Governance* 9: 165-173.

Hillman, A. and Dalziel, T. 2003. Boards of directors and firm performance: Integrating agency and resource dependence perspectives. *The Academy of Management Review* 28 (3): 383-396.

Judge, W., Naoumova, I., and Koutzevol, N. 2003. Corporate governance and firm performance in Russia: An empirical study. *Journal of World Business* 38: 385-396.

Kiel, C. and Nicholson, G. 2003. Board composition and corporate performance: How the Australian experience informs contrasting theories of corporate governance. *Corporate Governance: An International Review* 11 (3): 189-205.

Perry, T. and Shivdasani, A. 2005. Do boards affect performance? Evidence from corporate restructuring. *Journal of Business* 78: 1403–1431.

Vance, S. 1983. *Corporate leadership: boards, directors, and strategy.* New York: McGraw Hill Book Co.

Wier, C., Laing, D., and McKnight, P. 2003. An empirical analysis of the impact of corporate governance mechanisms on the performance of the UK firms. *Working paper*.

Yermack, D. 1996. Higher market valuation of companies with a small board of directors. *Journal of Financial Economics* 40: 185–211.

Zahra, S. and Pearce, J. 1989. Boards of Directors and Corporate Financial Performance: A Review and Integrative Model. *Journal of Management* 15 (2): 291–334.

Chapter 6

CORPORATE GOVERNANCE AND INTERNAL CONTROL MATERIAL WEAKNESSES

An entity's internal control system is characterized as a process that is implemented and managed by the management and other personnel within the entity, and the status of this system is reported to the entity's board of directors. The purpose of this system is to provide reasonable assurance regarding the reliability of the financial reports of the firm. Ashbaugh-Skaife, Collins, Kinney, and LaFond (2008) argue that better internal control reduces unintentional and intentional misstatements in financial statements as well as provides more accurate information for the day-to-day business operations inside the organizations. Likewise, weak internal control systems introduce noise and/or bias into accounting measurements, which can reduce the quality of both internally and externally reported accounting numbers. In this chapter, we review literature on the association between corporate governance mechanisms and the quality of internal control, which in turn affects the quality of financial reporting. We find that research in this stream is centered on SOX 2002, Sections 302 and 404, and unplanned consequences on internal control quality, firm value, costs of capital, audit process, and stock prices.

DETERMINANTS OF INTERNAL CONTROL DEFICIENCY

An extensive body of research investigates the determinants of internal control weaknesses and more specifically, material weaknesses. Doyle et al. (2007b) find that material weaknesses are more common among firms that are smaller, younger, financially weaker, more complex, growing rapidly, or undergoing restructuring. These characteristics appear to impact whether the firm is likely to experience an entity-wide or account-specific material weakness. On the other hand, firms with account specific internal control deficiencies tend to be larger, older, financially healthier, more complex, and growing more quickly than firms that demonstrate entity-wide control weaknesses. Thus, it appears that a firm's investment in IT and internal controls can be used as a measure of internal control risk (i.e., the higher the investment in IT and internal controls, the stronger the internal control system). Likewise, the lower the investment in internal controls, the higher the likelihood of internal control deficiencies.

Internal control risk factors can be explained by changes in organizational structure. For example, firms that have recently changed their organizational structure through mergers and acquisitions are more likely to experience internal control deficiencies due to differences of cultures and internal control systems. Further, to the extent that such firms are unable to successfully integrate their internal control systems, the risk of internal control weaknesses increases.

Theoretically, an effective information system should assure the effectiveness and efficiency of operations, the reliability of financial reporting, and compliance with applicable laws and regulations. An internal control deficiency (ICD) exists when the design or operation of a control system does not allow management or employees to *prevent* and/or *detect* errors or misstatements on a timely basis. Ashbaugh-Skaife, Collins, Kinney, and LaFond (2008) argue that better internal control reduces unintentional and intentional misstatements in financial statements, and provides more accurate information for the day-to-day business operations inside an organization. There are three types of internal control weaknesses. Listed in increasing order of rigor, these internal control weaknesses are control deficiencies, significant deficiencies, and material weaknesses (Bryan and Lilien, 2005). Ogneva, Subramanyam, and Raghunandan (2007) examine whether the type of weakness affects the association between the internal control weakness and the cost of equity. They classify internal control weaknesses into different categories that include: presence of multiple weaknesses, presence of personnel problems, presence of governance issues, presence of accounting/information systems-related problems, presence of systemic problems, presence of accounting restatements, and late filers (i.e., delayed filing their Section 404 reports for at least six months following the fiscal yearend). Overall, they find that some of these categories have higher costs of equity than other control firms in univariate tests, but none of these categories have significantly different costs of equity in multiple regressions, both as of June 2004 and June 2006.

In general, firms that report ICDs have more complex operations, are more likely to be involved in mergers and acquisitions, are more likely to have more investors, have fewer resources to invest in internal control, and have higher chances of auditor resignation. Ashbaugh-Skaife, Collins, and Kinney (2007) find that ICD firms are more likely to be exposed to prior SEC enforcement actions and financial restatement, use a dominant audit firm, and have more concentrated ownership. Likewise, Doyle, Ge, and McVay (2007b) find that the determinants of firms disclosing material weaknesses are that these firms tend to be smaller, younger, financially weaker, more complex, growing rapidly, or undergoing restructuring. Doyle et al. (2007b) suggest that these determinants vary according to the reasons for the material weakness. In other words, each firm has its own unique set of internal control features. Also, results suggest that firms that report account-specific weaknesses tend to be larger, older, financially healthier, have more complex and diversified business operations and are growing more rapidly than firms that report company-level weaknesses. Firms with company-wide problems apparently do not have either the resources or the experience to maintain a good control system.

Doyle et al. (2007b) also examine the relationship between accruals quality (as measured by the extent to which accruals are realized as cash flows) and internal control deficiencies, using a sample of firms that disclosed at least one internal control material weakness. The compelling reason to study material internal control weaknesses is that such weaknesses signal a potentially weak control environment that may allow management to engage in earnings management or earnings manipulation, resulting in poor accrual quality. Findings of Doyle et al. (2007b) indicate that firms with material weaknesses in internal control tend to have lower accruals quality, with especially poor accruals quality for company-level internal control weaknesses (as opposed to account specific internal control weaknesses).

Ge and McVay (2005) argue that material weaknesses are associated with inadequate accounting resources with respect to revenue recognition policies and segregation of duties among employees. In general, Ge and McVay (2005) find that disclosure of a material weakness is positively related to business complexity and presence of foreign currency translation and negatively related to firm size and profitability. In the same year, Bryan and Lilien (2005) investigate the characteristics of firms with material weaknesses in internal control post SOX 2002, Section 404 and find that firms with material weaknesses are smaller, worse performers, and have higher betas (risk factor), suggesting a higher discount by the market for these firms. Bronson, Carcello, and Raghunandan (2006) investigate the characteristics of med-sized firms issuing a voluntary Management Report on Internal Control (MRIC) based on a sample of 397 firms in 1998 prior to SOX 2002 Section 302. Results suggest that MRIC is more likely for larger firms that have an audit committee that meets more often, have a greater level of institutional ownership, and have more rapid income growth. This voluntary disclosure was less likely for firms with more rapid sales growth. Also, none of these MRIC mentioned material weaknesses. However, those firms that voluntarily disclosed information regarding internal control did not disclose information related to the effectiveness of their internal control systems that might be of interest to investors and various stakeholders.

SOX 2002, Section 302 and Internal Control Weaknesses

Beneish, Billings, and Hodder (2008) document a negative stock price reaction to internal control weakness disclosures using a short-window design under both Section 302 and Section 404. They argue that this negative stock price reaction attributes to lowered earnings' expectations and increased cost of equity. However, they document no significant stock price or cost-of-equity effects associated with Section 404 disclosures. Therefore, it is possible that internal control deficiencies could have cost-of-equity implications that were not apparent in prior research. In line with Beneish et al. (2008), Hammersley, Myers, and Shakespeare (2008) investigate the market reaction to disclosure of internal control material weaknesses under Section 302. They find that the market negatively reacts to internal control weakness disclosures and this reaction depends on the magnitude of the internal control weakness.

Ashbaugh-Skaife, Collins, and Kinney (2007) study the determinants of ICDs prior to SOX 2002, Section 404 and post SOC 302 and hence develop expectations of internal control problems. They investigate the economic factors that result in a firm's internal control risk and management's incentives to report and discover this control failure prior to SOX 2002, Section 404 and after the implementation of SOX 2002 Section 302. They used a sample of 326 firms with fiscal year-end December 31, 2004, with disclosed SOX 2002, Section 404 material weaknesses in their 10K filed. These authors suggest that the following economic factors resulted in internal control failure: (1) the complexity of the firm's operations, (2) the existence of recent organizational changes such as mergers and acquisitions, (3) audit resignation, (4) sales growth, (5) firm losses, and (6) the availability of resources for internal control.

Likewise, Doyle et al. (2007b) examine the determinants for material weakness of internal control for both pre-SOX 2002, Section 302 and post-SOX 2002, Section 404. They investigate whether material weaknesses in internal control are associated with firm size, firm age, financial health, financial reporting complexity, rapid growth, restructuring charges, and corporate governance. Doyle et al. (2007b) suggest that certain types of ICWs are more extreme than others. There are two types of material weaknesses: (1) Account-specific material weaknesses (not severe in terms of affecting the reliability of financial statements), and (2) Company-level material weaknesses (more severe in terms of affecting the reliability of financial statements). The sample includes 779 firms that disclosed material weaknesses from August 2002 to 2005. The dependent variable in this study is the probability of material weaknesses in internal control. The independent variables are firm size, firm age, financial health, financial reporting complexity, rapid growth, restructuring charges, and corporate governance measures (i.e., audit, board of directors, charter/bylaws, director education, executive and director compensation, ownership, and progressive practices).

SOX 2002: Section 404 and Internal Control Weaknesses

Ogneva, Subramanyam, and Raghunandan (2007) find that firms with internal control weaknesses post SOX 2002, Section 404 have higher implied cost of equity capital. They study 2,515 firms that filed first-time Section 404 reports (346 filed adverse opinions and 2,169 filed clean reports from November 2004 to January 2006). The authors first observed that firms with internal control deficiencies have higher cost of equity capital, but this cost of equity capital is not significantly associated with internal control weaknesses after controlling for firm characteristics and analysts' forecast bias.

Similarly, Krishnan and Visvanathan (2007) study the role of audit committees and auditors in the reporting of internal control deficiencies post SOX 2002. They used a sample of firms that reported internal control deficiencies post SOX 2002, Section 404, and assess the characteristics of audit committees and auditors for these firms. They find that a higher number of meetings of the audit committee, lower proportion of 'financial experts' in the audit committee, and more auditor changes characterize firms that report weaknesses in their internal controls compared to firms with no weaknesses. Also, prior restatements of financial statements are higher for firms that report weaknesses in internal controls. These results obtain after controlling for a variety of firm characteristics such as complexity of operations, profitability, and growth.

In contrast to Krishnan and Visvanathan (2007), Hoitash, Hoitash and Bédard (2009) investigate the relationship between corporate governance and internal control deficiency pre and post SOX 2002, Section 404. They find that stronger corporate governance is not associated with better internal controls under Section 302, but is negatively associated with material weakness disclosure under section 404. However, Cohen, Gaynor, Krishnamoorthy and Wright (2007) argue that size, financial strength, and operational complexity are the firm specific characteristics that motivate the firm to have a strong internal control system.

In line with Beneish et al. (2008), Gupta and Nayar (2006) investigate whether the application of the SOX 2002, Section 404 and its mandated requirements of disclosing internal control material weaknesses convey value-relevant information to stock equity. They use voluntary disclosures made by the Securities and Exchange Commission registrants and find that internal control weakness disclosures are significant, value-relevant information to the capital markets given that such disclosures are associated with a negative stock price reaction. This reaction is mitigated when management disclosed specific remediation steps taken to correct the reported internal control material weakness. Also, the price reaction is less negative for firms employing a Big-4 auditing firm as their external auditors, and firms with larger current liabilities relative to total assets. This finding suggests that internal control weaknesses might trigger a debt ratings review, which might increase borrowing cost and default risk.

Audit quality and audit committees also affect the quality of internal control systems. In this vein, Krishnan (2005) examines the association between audit committee quality (such as size, independence, and expertise) and the quality of corporate internal control (by using a dummy variable for the presence or absence of internal control problems). She used a sample of 128 firms over the years 1997 through 2000. Results are consistent with the importance of quality for an audit committee in terms of both independence and financial expertise. The results indicate that independent audit committee members and audit committee members with financial expertise are highly associated with less likelihood of internal control problems.

CONSEQUENCES OF SOX 2002 ON INTERNAL CONTROL SYSTEMS

SOX 2002 effects may go beyond the normal day-to-day operations of a firm. Gupta and Nayar (2006) suggest that the disclosure of internal control weaknesses might trigger a debt ratings review, which might increase borrowing cost and default risk. Relatedly, Beneish, Billings, and Hodder (2008) document an increase in audit fees due to the internal control reporting requirements of SOX 2002, based in part on the increase in billable hours. Moreover, anecdotal evidence suggests that auditor resignation in the year prior to the disclosure of the internal control deficiency could signal financial distress of the firm.

Moreover, SOX 2002 creates threats to small and medium sized enterprises since these firms often rely more on manual controls as opposed to automated controls. Further, the cost of 404 compliance could hinder IT investment and business process re-design. Another threat identified by Ashbaugh-Skaife's, Collins, Kinney, and LaFond (2008), is that firms with internal control deficiencies have lower quality accruals (a measure of reliable financial statements). This result suggests that internal control weaknesses result in unintentional errors and noise in accruals. It is documented in this study as well that when auditors confirm remediation of reported internal control deficiencies, accrual quality increases relative to firms that do not remediate their internal control deficiencies. Overall, results suggest that the quality of internal control affects the quality of accruals.

Likewise, Bronson, Carcello, and Raghunandan (2006) investigate the characteristics of medium-sized firms issuing voluntary management reports on internal control (MRIC), based on a sample of 397 firms in 1998 prior to SOX 2002. Results suggest that MRIC is more likely for larger firms that have an audit committee that meets more often, have a greater level of institutional ownership, and have more rapid income growth. This voluntary disclosure was less likely for firms with more rapid sales growth. The internal control regulations also impacted the outsourced and supply chain related activities since management must assess the internal controls of the partner organization as they relate to activities affecting that company. However, SOX 2002 enhanced transparency, improved corporate governance, resulted in better business processes and financial statements, and enhanced an organization's enterprise risk management. Results suggest that SOX 2002 improved enterprise risk management.

Table 3. Corporate Governance and Internal Control Material Weaknesses

Study	Sample	Corporate Governance Measures	Control Variables	Firm Value Measures	Findings
Hoitash, Hoitash and Bédard (2009)	5480 firm years: November 1994-May 2006	Corporate governance	Company size, financial health, complexity, business changes, industry risk, auditor type, auditor change	Internal control deficiency	Stronger corporate governance is not associated with better internal controls under Section 302 but negatively associated with material weakness disclosure under section 404
Beneish, Billings, and Hodder (2008)	336 firms: 1998-2003	Internal control weakness disclosures using a short-window design under both Section 302 and Section 404	Industry, time, total assets	Stock price	Negative stock price reaction to internal control weakness disclosures; no significant stock price or cost-of-equity effects associated with Section 404 disclosures
Hammersley, Myers, and Shakespeare (2008)	358 firm years: 1993-2005	Disclosure of internal control material weaknesses under SOX 2002, Section 302	Management announced news in 8K	Stock price	Market negatively reacts to internal control weakness disclosure and this reaction depends on magnitude of internal control weakness
Doyle, Ge, and McVay (2007b)	705 firms: August 2002-November 2005	Internal control deficiencies	Losses, sales volatility, CFO volatility, total assets, operating cycle, firm age, segments, extreme sales growth, restructuring charge	Accruals quality	Firms with material weaknesses in internal control tend to have lower accruals quality, especially for company-level internal control weaknesses (as opposed to account specific internal control weaknesses)
Ogneva, Subramanyam, and Raghunandan (2007)	2,515 firms: November 2004 - January 2006	The period post SOX 2002, Section 404	Earnings growth, book to market ratio,mergers and acquisitions, loss firms, restructuring, firm age	Internal control weakness, cost of equity capital	None of these categories of IC material weaknesses have significantly different costs of equity

Table 3. Corporate Governance and Internal Control Material Weaknesses (cont.)

Study	Sample	Corporate Governance Measures	Control Variables	Firm Value Measures	Findings
Krishnan and Visvanathan (2007)	118 firms: 2004-2005	Audit committees and auditors	Profitability, complexity, growth, organizational changes	Internal control deficiencies	A higher number of meetings of the audit committee, lower proportion of 'financial experts' in audit committee, and more auditor changes characterize firms that report weaknesses in internal controls compared to firms with no weaknesses
Cohen, Gaynor, Krishnamoorthy, and Wright (2007)	Survey of available research	Auditor communications with audit committees and boards of directors	None	Financial reporting quality, internal control, auditor's performance	SOX 2002 increased responsibility of audit committee, expanded dialogue between external auditor and audit committee
Bronson, Carcello, and Raghunandan (2006)	397 firms: 1998	Characteristics of medium-sized firms issuing voluntary management report on internal control (MRIC)	Firm specific characteristics	Voluntary management report on internal control	MRIC is more likely for larger firm that has an audit committee that meets more often, has a greater level of institutional ownership, and has more rapid income growth; voluntary disclosure less likely for firms with more rapid sales growth
Gupta and Nayar (2006)	90 firms: November 2003 - July 2004	Application of SOX 2002, Section 404 and its mandated requirements of disclosing internal control material weakness	Event studymethodology tocontrol for other confounding events around the disclosure of internal control material weaknesses	Stock prices	Disclosure of internal control material weaknesses is associated with negative stock price reaction; however, disclosure of remediation by management mitigates negative stock reaction
Krishnan (2005)	128 firms: 1997-2000	Audit committee quality (size, independence, expertise)	Auditor industry, tenure, type, firm growth, size, industry	Presence or absence of internal control problems	Independent audit committee and audit committee with financial expertise are highly associated with less likelihood of internal control problems

REFERENCES

Ashbaugh-Skaife, H., Collins, D., and Kinney, W. 2007. The discovery and reporting of internal control deficiencies prior to SOX 2002-mandated audits. *Journal of Accounting and Economics* 44: 166-192.

______ , ______ , ______ , and LaFond, R. 2008. The effect of SOX 2002 internal control deficiencies and their remediation on accrual quality. *The Accounting Review* 83 (1): 217-250.

Beneish, M., Billings, M., and Hodder, L. 2008. Internal control weaknesses and information uncertainty. *The Accounting Review* 83 (3): 665-704.

Bronson, S., Carcello, J., and Raghunandan, K. 2006. Firm characteristics and voluntary management reports on internal control. *Auditing: A Journal of Practice & Theory* 25 (2): 25-39.

Bryan, S. and S. Lilien. 2005. Characteristics of Firms with material weaknesses in internal control: An assessment of section 404 of Sarbanes Oxley. Working paper available at SSRN: http://ssrn.com/abstract=682363.

Cohen, J., Gaynor, L., Krishnamoorthy, G. and Wright, A. 2007. Auditor communications with the audit committee and the board of directors: Policy recommendations and opportunities for future research. *Accounting Horizons* 21 (2): 165–187.

Doyle, J., Ge, W., and McVay, S. 2007b. Determinants of weaknesses in internal control over financial reporting. *Journal of Accounting and Economics* 44: 193–223.

Ge, W. and McVay, S. 2005. The disclosure of material weaknesses in internal control after the Sarbanes-Oxley Act. *Accounting Horizons* 19 (3): 137–158.

Gupta, P. and Nayar, N. 2006. Information content of control deficiency disclosures under the Sarbanes-Oxley Act: An empirical investigation. *International Journal of Disclosure and Governance* 4 (1): 3-23.

Hammersley, J., Myers, L., and Shakespeare, C. 2008. Market reactions to the disclosure of internal control weaknesses and to the characteristics of those weaknesses under Section 302 of the Sarbanes Oxley Act of 2002. *Review of Accounting Studies* 13: 141–65.

Hoitash, R., Hoitash, U., and Bédard, J. 2009. Corporate Governance and Internal Control over Financial Reporting: A Comparison of Regulatory Regimes. *The Accounting Review* 8 (3): 839-867.

Krishnan, G. and Visvanathan, G. 2007. Reporting internal control deficiencies in the post-Sarbanes-Oxley era: The role of auditors and corporate governance. *International Journal of Auditing* 11: 73-90.

Ogneva, M., Subramanyam, K., and Raghunandan, K. 2007. Internal control weakness and cost of equity: Evidence from SOX 2002 Section 404 disclosures. *The Accounting Review* 82 (5): 1255-1297.

PART III. CORPORATE GOVERNANCE AND FINANCIAL REPORTING QUALITY

Chapter 7

Corporate Governance and Earnings Management

Financial Reporting Quality

High quality financial reporting has the potential to serve a number of important roles. For example, financial accounting information is a vital communication tool between managers (insiders) and various stakeholders (outsiders), and provides these outsiders financial data that helps them in making decisions about a firm's performance for a given period of time. Therefore, the information contained in year-end financial reports should accurately and fairly represent the truth about the firm's performance and the firm's value to reduce information asymmetry between managers and stakeholders. Financial accounting information can also play an important role in disciplining management if the information is transparent. Further, such transparency can help prevent management from expropriating stakeholders' resources, which in turn yields benefits to the economy. Financial accounting information can also serve as a tool for developing managerial incentive plans. Anecdotal evidence on the association between corporate governance mechanisms and financial reporting quality suggests that financial accounting information plays a major role in promoting efficient governance mechanisms by contributing to the information contained in stock prices. Likewise, strong corporate governance mechanisms provide greater control of the financial accounting process and improve the quality of financial reporting.

Corporate Governance and Financial Reporting Quality

Financial reporting quality can be measured by using many proxies, such as: earnings timeliness, accruals quality, earnings restatements, internal control quality (as previously shown), and earnings informativness (the returns-earnings association). In this section, we summarize research on the association between financial reporting quality and corporate governance mechanisms. For example, Bushman, Chen, Engel, and Smith (2004) use earnings timeliness to proxy for the intrinsic governance usefulness of accounting information, which is defined as the extent to which current accounting earnings incorporate current economic income or value-relevant information. They find that only a small portion of the cross-sectional variation in earnings timeliness can be explained by firms' growth opportunities, return volatility, size, industry, geographic diversification, and past performance. As predicted, they find that ''strong'' governance systems characterized by high ownership concentration, strong directors' and executives' equity-based incentives, and the strong reputation (i.e., quality) of outside directors, vary inversely with the timeliness of earnings. In addition, they find evidence that ownership concentration and directors' equity-based incentives increase, as predicted, with firm complexity. However, board size and the percentage of inside directors did not vary significantly with either the timeliness of earnings or firm complexity. They also explore whether the relative importance of accounting numbers in equity valuation appears to matter in the determination of corporate governance systems of large public companies in the U.S. Evidence supports the notion that firm-specific timeliness metrics capture meaningful differences across large public U.S. companies in the information properties of accounting numbers. Furthermore, the authors investigate how ownership concentration, directors' and executive's incentives, and board structure vary with: (1) earnings timeliness and (2) organizational complexity (measured as geographic and/or product line diversification). They find that ownership concentration, directors' and executives' equity-based incentives, and outside directors' reputations vary inversely with earnings timeliness, and that ownership concentration, and directors' equity-based incentives increase with firm complexity. However, board size and the percentage of inside directors do not vary significantly with earnings timeliness or firm complexity.

Likewise, Niu's (2006) study examines the association between corporate governance mechanisms and the quality of accounting earnings using a sample of 519 firm-year observations for the accrual model and 528 firm-year observations for the returns-earnings association model for the years 2001-2004. The quality of earnings is measured by two methods: the accounting-based measure of earnings management and the market-based measure of earnings informativeness. The corporate governance mechanisms tested include: board composition, management shareholding, shareholders' rights, and the extent of disclosure of governance practices. The author find that governance quality is negatively associated with the level of abnormal accruals (corporate governance proxy) and positively influences the return-earnings association. These results suggest that the Canadian regulators' attempts to strengthen corporate governance mechanisms did provide greater monitoring of the financial accounting process and improved the quality of abnormal accruals.

Agrawal and Chadh (2005) examine the relationship between corporate governance mechanisms (such as auditors' independence, financial expertise of boards, and audit committees) and the likelihood of restatement in financial reporting. The authors analyze a sample of 159 U.S. public companies that restated their earnings in either 2000 or 2001 and an industry size-matched control sample of 159 non-restating firms. The results suggest no relationship between the probability of restatement and corporate governance mechanisms implied in board independence, audit committee independence, or auditor conflicts. However, Agrawal and Chadh (2005) find that the probability of restatement is significantly lower in companies whose boards or audit committees include an independent director with financial expertise, but higher in companies in which the CEO belongs to the founding family.

Agency theory suggests that managers usually make trade-offs between costs and benefits of disclosure, and they may have incentives to distort disclosure policy. Ajinkya, Bhojrai, and Sengupta (2005) argue that corporate governance mitigates this effect and reduces the distortion of disclosure by managers. In their study, these authors investigate the effect of institutional ownership and board of directors' composition on the properties of management earnings forecasts. Overall, they find that corporate governance has a favorable effect in terms of reducing management' forecast errors. In the same line of reasoning, Karamanou and Vefeas (2005) examine how corporate boards and audit committees are associated with voluntary financial disclosure practices (management earnings forecasts). The authors use a sample of 275 firms that announced 1,621 forecasts in 1,274 firm-year observations between

1995 and 2000. Results confirm that in firms with more effective board and audit committee structures, managers are more likely to make or update earnings forecasts. Results also suggest that effective corporate governance is associated with higher financial disclosure quality.

Future research might focus on the association between specific components of financial statements and corporate governance mechanisms to promote financial reporting quality. Specifically, as the marketplace continues to become more interconnected, researchers might focus on various components of the financial statements to discern important differences (or similarities) across these components with respect to the corporate governance mechanisms that are in place. Additional governance research is encouraged to explore more comprehensively the use of financial accounting information with respect to additional corporate control mechanisms.

Corporate Governance and Earnings Management

Earnings Management

Bushman and Smith (2001) define earnings management or manipulations as "information *suppression* mechanisms that tends to restrict the managers from taking certain actions that would maximize shareholder's wealth." Managers might manipulate earnings for a number of reasons. By manipulating earnings, managers might simply want to achieve predetermined earnings numbers to survive in the market, they might want to beat or meet analysts' expectations in an attempt to increase the market value of equity, or they might understate earnings in order to acquire a firm (known as management buyouts) or achieve tax savings. Also, Burgstahler and Eames (2003) find that analysts anticipate earnings management to avoid small losses and small earnings decreases. Alternatively, the firm might plan to merge with another company and afterwards managers tend to overstate earnings. Another possible explanation for earnings management is to beat "Wall Street's" earnings expectations each quarter. Actually, in 1998, the Securities and Exchange Commission Chairman blamed management for managing earnings and also blamed most of the involved parties in the process of preparing the financial statements, including auditors, analysts, and managers "*who are participating in a game of nods and winks.*" In fact, earnings management affects the quality of financial statements and can decrease investor's confidence in the accuracy and reliability of financial statements.

Consequences of Earnings Management on the Firm

Earnings management can have severe consequences on a firm, stakeholders, and interested parties who make their investment decisions based on the credibility of financial statements. Incorrect financial statements might also impact stock market efficiency that is influenced by the total information set available in the market. Accounting information is an important source of this flow of information. Taken together, earnings management might affect the whole economy and disturb overall economic growth. Anecdotal evidence suggests that boards that are comprised mostly of insiders are assumed to align the interest of management with their desired quality of financial reporting, which in turn hinders the boards' oversight and monitoring function over the management. This would increase the likelihood of earnings management. Likewise, the higher the number of outsiders on the board, the more independent the board would be from management, and the expectation is that the firm would produce higher quality financial reports with less earnings management. Doyle, Ge, and McVay (2007a) examine the relationship between accruals quality (as measured by the extent to which accruals are realized as cash flows) and internal control deficiencies, using a sample of firms that disclosed at least one material weakness. Material internal control weaknesses signal a potentially weak control environment that may allow management to engage in earnings management or earnings manipulation, resulting in poor accrual quality. Findings indicate that firms with material weaknesses in internal control tend to have lower accruals quality, with especially poor accruals quality for company-level internal control weaknesses (as opposed to account specific internal control weaknesses).

Earnings Management and Financial Crises

Is earnings management responsible for the current global financial crisis or is earnings management is one of the contributing factors to this crisis? Coffee (2005) investigates why corporate scandals occur so frequently in the U.S. and not as often in Europe, although both economies are subject to the same macroeconomic conditions.

Table 4. Corporate Governance and Financial Reporting Quality

Study	Sample	Corporate Governance Measures	Control Variables	Firm Value Measures	Findings
Agrawal and Chadh (2005)	159 US public companies that restated earnings: 2000 or 2001	Auditors' independence, financial expertise of boards, audit committees	Firm size, profitability, growth rates, financial leverage	The likelihood of restatement in financial reporting	No relationship between the probability of restatement and corporate governance mechanisms; probability of restatement is significantly lower in companies whose boards or audit committees include an independent director with financial expertise, but higher in companies where CEO belongs to founding family
Ajinkya, Bhojrai, and Sengupta (2005)	2934 annual forecasts: 1997-2002	Institutional ownership and board of directors' composition	Reg FD, standard deviation of analysts' forecasts, market value, auditor firm, litigation risk, loss firms	Properties of management earnings forecasts	Corporate governance has a favorable effect in terms of reducing managements' forecast errors
Karamanou and Vefeas (2005)	275 firms: 1995-2000	Corporate board, audit committees	Information environment using analysts following, firm size dispersion in analysts' forecasts; high tech industry	Voluntary financial disclosure practices (management earnings forecasts)	Firms with more effective board and audit committee structures are more likely to make or update earnings forecasts; effective corporate governance is associated with higher financial disclosure quality
Bushman, Chen, Engel, and Smith (2004)	784 firms: 1994-1997	Ownership concentration, strong directors' and executives' equity-based incentives, and strong reputation (i.e., quality) of outside directors	Firm's growth as a composite measure, CEO tenure, firm age, market value of equity	Earnings timeliness, organizational complexity	Strong governance systems characterized by high ownership concentration, strong directors' and executives' equity-based incentives, and strong reputation (i.e., quality) of outside directors vary inversely with timeliness of earnings

Results of the study suggest that the structure of share ownership determines the nature of the fraud. In other words, dispersed ownership, such as that found in the U.S., creates managerial incentives to manage earnings while concentrated ownership, such as that found in Europe, is less vulnerable to earnings management. As a result, governance protections that work in one system may not work in the other. The presence of good corporate governance mitigates the asymmetric information between shareholders and managers and hence reduces management discretionary behavior and earnings management. However, results of the empirical investigation on the effect of the presence of strong corporate governance on firm's outcomes such as quality financial reporting (e.g., low earnings management, low restatement, strong internal control systems, and timeliness of accounting reporting) suggest that corporate governance does not curb earnings management (Weber, 2006). A possible explanation for the inconclusive evidence on the usefulness of corporate governance to limit fraud and corruption might be explained by stewardship theory. Stated differently, managers might be smoothing income or adjusting accruals to maximize returns for shareholders as an outcome of efficient contracting arising from incentive alignment (Weber, 2006). Underlying this latter premise, earnings management is not responsible for initiating the global financial crisis.

In 1998, SEC Chairman Levitt gave a famous speech[1] where he sharply criticized earnings management practices and pointed out that earnings management had become a "game" that weakened the credibility of financial reporting. An excerpt from Chairman Levitt states:

> "Seven months ago, I expressed concerns about selective disclosure. Through conference calls or embargoed press releases, analysts and institutional investors often hear about material news before it is made public. In the interval, there is a great deal of unusual trading. The practice had been going on for a long time. And, while everyone was aware of it, and most were extremely uncomfortable with it, few spoke out. As the investor's advocate, the SEC did and we will continue to do so.
>
> Well, today, I'd like to talk to you about another widespread, but too little-challenged custom: earnings management. This process has evolved over the years into what can best be characterized as a game among market participants. A game that, if not addressed soon, will have adverse consequences for America's financial reporting system. A game that runs counter to the very principles behind our market's strength and success.

[1] http://www.sec.gov/news/speech/speecharchive/1998/spch220.txt

> Increasingly, I have become concerned that the motivation to meet Wall Street earnings expectations may be overriding common sense business practices. Too many corporate managers, auditors, and analysts are participants in a game of nods and winks. In the zeal to satisfy consensus earnings estimates and project a smooth earnings path, wishful thinking may be winning the day over faithful representation.
>
> As a result, I fear that we are witnessing an erosion in the quality of earnings, and therefore, the quality of financial reporting. Managing may be giving way to manipulation; Integrity may be losing out to illusion.
>
> Many in corporate America are just as frustrated and concerned about this trend as we, at the SEC, are. They know how difficult it is to hold the line on good practices when their competitors operate in the gray area between legitimacy and outright fraud.
>
> A gray area where the accounting is being perverted; where managers are cutting corners; and, where earnings reports reflect the desires of management rather than the underlying financial performance of the company.
>
> Tonight, I want to talk about why integrity in financial reporting is under stress and explore five of the more common accounting gimmicks we've been seeing. Finally, I will outline a framework for a financial community response to this situation….".

According to Munter (1999), the five most important earnings management tools that the Securities and Exchange Commission was concerned about in 1998 are: "big bath" restructuring charges where companies use their restructuring charges to clean up their balance sheets, creative acquisition accounting (in-process R&D and write-off), cookie jar reserves, immaterial misapplications of accounting principles, and premature recognition of revenue. Despite the fact that the U.S. legal environment is characterized by strong outside investor protection and good corporate governance structure, there is evidence of earnings management (Wright, Shaw, and Guan, 2006; Healy and Wahlen, 1999; and Weber, 2006).

Corporate Governance and Earnings Management

Theoretically, the presence of good corporate governance mitigates management discretionary behavior. However, results of prior research (Weber, 2006) suggest that good corporate governance does not curb earnings management. Wright, Shaw, and Guan (2006) investigate the occurrence of earnings management in the U.S. and the UK. Both countries are characterized as having strong corporate governance structures. Wright, Shaw, and Guan (2006) use a sample of 92 UK firms from 1997-2002 and 63 U.S. firms from 1981-1988. Prior research in international accounting and cultural differences suggests a difference in corporate governance structures between the UK and the U.S. that could differentially impact earnings management in these countries. Results of Wright et al. (2006) suggest that managers in both countries manage their earnings prior to management buyouts (MBOs) and that earnings management was even more aggressive in the U.S. than in the UK. However, the sample of this study was drawn from a specific group (MBOs) and this limited sample might either overstate or understate the results due to bias in research settings. One possible explanation, beyond the failure of corporate governance to curb managerial opportunistic behavior, might be stewardship theory. Stated differently, managers might be smoothing income or adjusting accruals to maximize returns for shareholders as an outcome of efficient contracting arising from incentive alignment (Weber, 2006). Therefore, we classify research in this area into two main streams; a stream suggesting that corporate governance curbs earnings management and another stream, proposed by the opponents to corporate governance, suggesting that corporate governance is more like a context based system that failed to curb earnings management practices. In this section we will discuss the extant literature on these two streams.

Corporate Governance Curbs Earnings Management

Ebrahim (2007) examines the relation between earnings management and corporate governance mechanisms, such as the activity of the board and the audit committee, in addition to institutional ownership, and audit quality. He uses a sample of manufacturing firms over the years 1999-2000. This study is different from prior research in that it uses a larger sample and different models to measure earnings management. It also tests the interactions between both the board and audit committee independence and their activity. It assumes that both independent boards and audit committees restrain earnings management activities when independent boards and audit committees are more active and meet more frequently during the year. Results indicate that earnings management was negatively associated with both board and audit committee independence and there was a stronger negative association when the audit committee was more active.

Weber (2006) investigates whether executive wealth sensitivity to stock price fluctuations is used to manage earnings. The author used a sample of 475 chief executive officers from 410 randomly selected Standard and Poor's 1500 firms as of January 1995, to examine the relation between executive stock-based compensation, corporate governance, and earnings management. Results suggest a positive relationship between CEO wealth sensitivity and abnormal accrual usage and that the relation is consistent with income smoothing. However, governance does not significantly influence the association between CEO stock-based wealth sensitivity and earnings smoothing. These findings have implications for both compensation plans and policy implications because they suggest that reliance on these standards as deterrents to earnings management may be valid.

Mir and Seboui (2006) test whether earnings management and governance mechanisms link the disparity between accounting values [economic value added (EVA)] and market value [created shareholder value (CSV)]. In other words, the purpose of this study was to analyze the differences between EVA and CSV. The sample consists of 247 firms for the period 1998–2004. Results show a non-significant relationship between EVA and CSV and a positive association between the difference (CSV-EVA) and discretionary accruals as a proxy of earnings management. The results also suggest that some governance mechanisms can reduce the gap between CSV and EVA whereas others can increase it. Finally, the results reveal that the different cases of convergence and divergence between CSV and EVA can be explained by governance mechanisms and earnings management.

Davidson, Goodwin-Stewart, and Kent (2005) investigate the relationship between the strength of a firm's internal governance structure and earnings management using a sample of 434 Australian firms for the financial year ending in 2000. The study is based on the assumption that earnings management is systematically reduced by the strength of internal corporate governance mechanisms, including the board of directors, the audit committee, the internal audit function and the choice of external auditor. Results indicate that a majority of non-executive directors on the board and on the audit committee were significantly associated with a lower likelihood of earnings management (measured by absolute level of discretionary accruals). However, the voluntary establishment of an internal audit function and the choice of auditor were not significantly related to a reduction in the level of discretionary accruals.

Klien (2002) examines whether the magnitude of abnormal accruals (the proxy for earnings management) was related to audit committee independence using a sample of 692 publicly traded U.S. firm-years for 1992–1993. This paper was motivated by assertions made by the SEC, the NYSE, and the NASDAQ that there was a positive association between earnings management and poor corporate governance mechanisms. Results suggest a negative relation between audit committee independence and abnormal accruals. A negative relation was also found between board independence and abnormal accruals, which was more apparent when either the board or the audit committee was comprised of a minority of outside directors. Accordingly, boards that are independent from the CEO are more effective in monitoring the corporate financial accounting process and exercising corporate governance.

CORPORATE GOVERNANCE DOES NOT CURB EARNINGS MANAGEMENT

Hsu and Koh (2005) examine how the corporate governance role of institutional investors is associated with their portfolio firms' accruals management. The authors use institutional ownership to proxy for institutional investor types, in which lower ownership proxied for transient institutions (more likely to vote with their feet, i.e., exit), and higher ownership proxied for transient long-term oriented institutions (more likely to be actively involved in their portfolio firms' governance, i.e., voice). The authors use a sample of 201 firm-year observations for their study and find that temporary and long-term oriented institutions co-exist and have differential effects on portfolio firms' earnings management. Temporary institutions are associated with upward accruals management, while long-term oriented institutions control upward accruals management. These results suggest that long-term oriented institutions can act as a corporate governance mechanism to mitigate aggressive earnings management. Overall, the authors find that the association between institutional ownership and earnings management was context dependent, suggesting complex associations between institutional ownership and earnings management strategies.

Table 5. Corporate Governance and Earnings Management

Study	Sample	Corporate Governance Measures	Control Variables	Firm Value Measures	Findings
Ebrahim (2007)	1999-2000	Activity of board and audit committee; institutional ownership, audit quality	Firm's prior performance, firm size, auditor, market to book ratio	Earnings management as measured by abnormal discretionary accruals	Earnings management negatively associated with board and audit committee independence; stronger negative association when audit committee more active
Mir and Seboui (2006)	247 firms: 1998–2004	Created shareholder value	Firm size, auditor, R&D, market to book ratio	Earnings management as measured by discretionary accruals	governance mechanisms and earnings management explain disparity between Economic Value added and Created Shareholder Value
Weber (2006)	410 S&P firms: 1996-1999	Governance score composed of board structure, ownership structure, institutional environment	Executive bonus, return on assets, market value of equity, market to book ratio, debt to total assets, firm risk	CEO sensitivity to stock price fluctuations, abnormal accruals	Corporate governance does not significantly influence the association between CEO sensitivity to stock price fluctuations and abnormal accruals earnings management
Wright, Shaw, and Guan (2006)	92 UK firms: 1997-2002 63 US firms: 1981-1988	Country's legal environment	Whether the firm undergoes MBO, industry, fiscal year, total assets	Earnings management measured by discretionary accruals	Managers in both countries manage their earnings prior to management buyouts (MBOs) and this was even more aggressive in the US than in the UK.; sample was drawn from a specific group (MBOs) - earnings management might differ if tested under different research setting

Table 5. Corporate Governance and Earnings Management (cont.)

Study	Sample	Corporate Governance Measures	Control Variables	Firm Value Measures	Findings
Davidson, Goodwin-Stewart, and Kent (2005)	434 Australian firms: 2000	Board of directors, audit committee	Leverage, size, change in earnings, market to book ratio, extreme performance	Earnings management as measured by absolute level of discretionary accruals	Majority of non-executive directors on board and on audit committee were significantly associated with a lower likelihood of earnings management
Hsu and Koh (2005)	201 firms	Institutional ownership	Firm size, leverage, audit quality, managerial ownership, lagged total accruals, cash flow from operations, industry membership, year	Earnings management as measured by discretionary accruals	Association between institutional ownership and earnings management was context dependent, suggesting complex associations between institutional ownership and earnings management strategies
Klien (2002)	692 U.S. firm-years: 1992–1993	Audit committee independence	Factors that might be correlated to abnormal accruals or audit committees	Magnitude of abnormal accruals	Negative relation between audit committee independence and abnormal accruals; negative relation between board independence and abnormal accruals, which was more apparent when either the board or the audit committee was comprised of a minority of outside directors

To sum up, results of studies in this section suggest that earnings management might be systematically reduced by a number of both firm-level and country-level corporate governance mechanisms. For example, boards that are independent of the CEO provide a stronger corporate governance environment for the firm and independent boards are more effective in monitoring the corporate financial accounting process. Equally important, effective corporate governance is associated with higher financial disclosure quality. Nevertheless, we find meaningful opportunities to continue research in this area. For example, the eXtensible Business Reporting Language (XBRL) was developed to improve the accuracy and reliability of financial information (www.xbrl.org). Cohen, Schiavina, and Servais (2005) claim that XBRL's potential benefits include increased efficiency and transparency of financial information (i.e., more reusable digital reports, more types of information available on a more frequent basis, improved internal reporting, and a better controls environment). Based on these claims, researchers might wish to explore the types and extent of earnings management in companies (intra-country and inter-country) that have adopted XBRL technology for reporting financial information. The expectation is that the increased transparency of company information would be negatively and significantly associated with earnings management. Empirical tests of this expectation should be very interesting for the management of these companies, regulators, and investors. Another area of possible future research might be the evaluation of different accounting treatments that might be considered as earnings management (or earnings smoothing) schemes by management of a firm. The extant literature on earnings management predominantly focuses on discretionary accruals as a proxy of earnings management. Are other treatments as useful or more useful in predicting earnings management? Which corporate governance mechanisms are negatively and significantly associated with these various accounting treatments, i.e, which corporate governance mechanisms are most useful in mitigating earnings management?

REFERENCES

Agrawal, A. and Chadh, S. 2005. Corporate governance and accounting scandals. *The Journal of Law and Economics* 48: 371–406.

Ajinkya, B., Bhojrai, S., and Sengupta, P. 2005. The association between outside directors, institutional investors, and the properties of management earnings forecasts. *Journal of Accounting Research* 43 (3): 343-376.

Burgstahler, D. and Eames, M. 2003. Earnings management to avoid losses and earnings decreases: are analysts fooled? *Contemporary Accounting Research* 20 (2): 53 – 294.

Bushman, R. and Smith, A. 2001. Financial accounting information and corporate governance. *Journal of Accounting and Economics* 32: 237-333.

______ , Chen, Q., Engel, E. and Smith, A. 2004. Financial accounting information, organizational complexity, and corporate governance systems. *Journal of Accounting and Economics* 37: 167-201.

Coffee, J. 2005. A theory of corporate scandals: Why the USA and Europe differ. *Oxford Review Of Economic Policy* 21 (2): 198-211.

Cohen, E., Schiavina, T., and Servais, O. 2005. XBRL: The standardized business language for 21st century reporting and governance. *International Journal of Disclosure and Governance* 2 (4): 368-394.

Davidson, R. Goodwin-Stewart, J. and Kent, P. 2005. Internal governance structures and earnings management. *Accounting and Finance* 45: 241–267.

Doyle, J., Ge, W., and McVay, S. 2007a. Accruals quality and internal control over financial reporting. *The Accounting Review* 82 (5): 1141-1170

Ebrahim, A. 2007. Earnings management and board activity: An additional evidence. *Review of Accounting and Finance* 6 (1): 42-58.

Healy, P. and Wahlen, J. 1999. A review of earnings management literature and its implications for standard setting. *Accounting Horizons* 13: 365-383.

Hsu, G. and Koh, P. 2005. Does the presence of institutional investors influence accruals management? Evidence from Australia. *Corporate Governance* 13 (6): 809-823.

Karamanou, I. and Vafeas, N. 2005. The association between corporate boards, audit committees, and management earnings forecasts: An empirical analysis. *Journal of Accounting Research* 43 (3): 453-486.

Klein, A. 2002. Audit committee, board of director characteristics, and earnings management. *Journal of Accounting & Economics* 33: 375–400.

Mir, A. and Seboui, S. 2006. Corporate governance and earnings management and the relationship between economic value added and created shareholder value. *Journal of Asset Management* 7 (3): 242-254.

Munter, P. 1999. SEC Sharply criticizes "Earnings Management" accounting. *The Journal of Corporate Accounting and Finance* 10 (2): 31-38.

Niu, F. 2006. Corporate governance and the quality of accounting earnings: A Canadian perspective. *International Journal of Managerial Finance* 2 (4): 302-327.

Weber, M. 2006. Sensitivity of executive wealth to stock price, corporate governance and earnings management. *Review of Accounting and Finance* 5 (4): 321-354.

Wright, C., Shaw, J., and Guan, L. 2006. Corporate governance and investor protection: Earnings management in the U.K. and U.S. *Journal of International Accounting Research* 5 (1): 25-40.

Chapter 8

CORPORATE GOVERNANCE AND FIRM VOLUNTARY DISCLOSURE

Healy and Palepu (2001) suggest that disclosure generally improves transparency and thus reduces information asymmetry between managers and outsiders. Information and agency problems typically hinder the efficient allocation of resources and hence disclosure helps mitigate these problems. We divide the literature on corporate governance and voluntary disclosure into two main streams of research: (1) corporate governance and management's earnings forecasts, and (2) corporate governance and analysts' earnings forecasts. We then discuss the methodologies, main thrust, and outcomes of these two main streams of research.

CORPORATE GOVERNANCE AND MANAGEMENT EARNINGS FORECASTS

Management Earnings Forecasts

Management Earnings Forecasts (MEFs) are primarily issued to either communicate private information to investors or guide analysts toward a beatable earnings target. Motives for voluntary disclosure include: 1. Capital market transaction (the theory is that investors' perception of a firm are important to corporate managers), 2. Corporate control contests (the theory is that BOD and investors hold managers accountable for current performance), 3. Stock compensation (the theory is that management stock-based compensation encourages managers to engage in voluntary disclosure), 4. Litigation cost (could be an incentive - depends on managers being forward looking or wanting to provide adequate and timely information to investors), 5. Proprietary costs (disclosure can damage managers' competitive position in the market), 6. Management talent signaling (talented managers are more likely to voluntarily disclose information to reveal their type).

Richardson, Teoh, and Wysocki (2004) set a framework of earnings guidance that is composed of five points: 1. The selling of stock usually occurs during a short window after earnings announcements. 2. Managers who have incentives to sell stock on either their personal account or behalf of the firm are more interested in short-term post-announcement stock price. 3. Managers influence analysts' forecasts through voluntary disclosure and analysts cooperate. 4. Analysts' forecasts are initially optimistic. 5. The market rewards firms that beat analysts' latest forecasts. Richardson, Teoh, and Wysocki (2004) also examine whether the walk down of analysts' forecasts from optimistic to pessimistic earnings forecasts are associated with management incentives to sell stock either through new equity issuance or options exercises and stock sales. They find that the walk-down to beatable earnings targets is more prevalent in the late 1990s, and when sellers of stock are insiders (selling of executive stock options), outsiders (issuing new equity) or net sellers (making profits).

Related, Matsumoto (2002) investigates managements' incentives to avoid negative earnings surprises. She contends that institutional investors are more conservative about the investments they make on behalf of individual investors. They bear portfolio performance in the short-term, the risk of judgment error owing to a diversified portfolio, and the need for a defensible measure for trading due to fiduciary responsibilities. Thus, they are more susceptible to negative earnings announcements. Overall, she finds that firms use both earnings management and forecast guidance to avoid negative earnings surprises. Firms with certain characteristics are more highly associated with one mechanism than the other. Similarly, Skinner (1994) provides support for firms' voluntary/discretionary disclosures of bad news. That is, managers have incentives to preempt large negative (but not large positive) earnings surprises by voluntarily disclosing that information early to avoid costly stockholders lawsuits. Managers voluntarily disclose earnings when their firms are doing well to distinguish their firm from their competition.

Corporate Governance and Management Earnings' Forecasts

Karamanou and Vafeas (2005) investigate the association between the strength of corporate governance (e.g., effective board and audit committee structure) and the occurrence, precision, and accuracy of management earnings forecasts for 275 Fortune 500 firms between 1995 and 2000. They provide empirical evidence supporting the argument that good corporate governance is associated with more accurate management earnings forecasts and these accurate forecasts are considered as favorable news by the market. However, Karamanou and Vafeas' (2005) study was executed prior to the enactment of SOX 2002. Hence we encourage researchers to replicate their study to determine whether SOX 2002 enhanced voluntary disclosure, reduced forecast errors, and revealed market appreciation in response to more transparent disclosure.

In criticizing the small sample of Karamanou and Vafeas' (2005) study, Ajinkya, Bhojraj, and Sengupta (2005) investigate the association between the properties of management earnings forecasts and corporate governance structure (e.g., board of directors and institutional ownership) for 1253 firms from 1997 to 2002. Ajinkya, Bhojraj, and Sengupta (2005) find that firms with outside directors and more institutional ownership (strong corporate governance structure) are more likely to issue accurate and frequent earnings forecasts. Moreover, they document a negative association between concentrated ownership (weak corporate governance structure) and forecasts' properties. The later association was less negative post Regulation Fair Disclosure in 1996, indicating that Regulation Fair Disclosure prohibited management from communicating private information to some selected stakeholders. In line with the results of Ajinkya, Bhojraj, and Sengupta (2005), Lim, Matolcsy, and Chow (2007) provide evidence on the positive association between board composition and voluntary disclosure. Moreover, Lim, Matolcsy, and Chow (2007) find that independent boards provide more valuable voluntary disclosure such as forward looking and strategic information.

Corporate Governance and Analysts' Forecasts

Analysts' Forecasts

Analysts' forecasts are recommendations of stocks to buy and sell, and forecasting earnings for individual firms. Research in this area is divided into two main streams – examination of properties of consensus (accuracy) analysts' forecasts, or examination of properties of individual analysts' forecasts. Analysts' optimism or error is apparent in the literature for many reasons, including internal pressure from analysts' firms (effects of forecasts on brokerage commissions and investment banking business), pressure from management of the companies that the analysts cover, pressure from institutional shareholders who are clients of the analysts, conflicts with analysts' personal investments, analysts' unintentional cognitive biases.

Analysts' earnings forecasts is an external corporate governance mechanism as discussed in chapter one. Hence, financial analysts, banks, brokerages, and institutional investors all play an important role in disciplining management of a firm by periodically following the firm and reporting estimates of firms' future earnings based on the financial analysts' expectations of the firms' performance. Therefore, analysts' earnings forecasts are also a pivotal tool in resolving the conflicts of interests between the management and shareholders and in reducing the agency costs underlying the corporate governance code and its subsequent provisions.

In general, researchers document more optimistic forecasts relative to pessimistic forecasts (Butler and Lang, 1991; Richardson, Teoh, and Wysocki, 2004; and Easterwood and Nutt, 1999). This prior research documents differences in analysts' forecast accuracy, although these studies typically do not attempt to explain why these differences exist. Moreover, results of this body of research on forecast accuracy are mixed. For example, Dreman and Berry (1995) suggest that forecast errors are less accurate than forecasts by time-series models, the errors are increasing over time, and that the analysts' forecasts are too optimistic. Brown (1996) provides evidence that analysts' forecast errors are within 3 percent of an appropriate benchmark (e.g., stock price) and that analysts' forecasts are better than those provided by sophisticated time-series models. Bulter and Lang (1991) support this previous conclusion and find no statistically significant evidence of differential analyst forecast accuracy. In this chapter, we outline the available evidence on the relationship between corporate governance and analysts' forecasts.

Why Does Analysts' Optimism/Error Exist?

Chang, Cho, and Shin (2007) argue that analysts are primarily interested in generating trading commissions, and are therefore hesitant to issue negative investment information (pessimism) because they fear jeopardizing potential investment banking business. Also, if they lose those investment opportunities, they are more likely to lose management communication as a source of valuable information to them. Anecdotal evidence suggests that analysts' are trying to improve market perceptions of the firms or are simply irrational in their earnings forecasts (Richardson, Teoh, and Wysocki, 2004.) Research suggests that analysts' optimism occurs usually over a long horizon. However, in the short-horizons, analysts tend to switch from optimism to pessimism to walk down their forecasts to a beatable earnings target (Richardson et al., 2004). Richardson et al. (2004) suggest that analysts do not process the publically available information (such as prior earnings, forecasts errors and revisions, and stock returns) wisely to produce unbiased earnings forecasts. The conclusion is that the results are mixed on the inefficiency or bias of analysts' earnings forecasts (Abarbanel and Lehavy, 2003).

Cowen, Groysbery, and Healy (2006) investigate which type of analyst firms make more optimistic forecasts and find that analysts at firms with underwriting and trading businesses are less optimistic or biased than analysts at brokerage houses. Cowen, Groysbery and Healy (2006) attribute analysts' optimism to trading activities used to fund research. Sedor (2002) provides an explanation for the unintentional optimism in analysts' earnings forecasts using a 2 x 2 between-subjects experimental design. She imputed analysts' optimism to analysts' reactions to managers' future plans. Consistent with the Sedor (2002), Kadous, Krische, and Sedor's (2006) use an experimental study to test whether the counter explanations reduce analysts' optimism. They base their study on the assumption that analysts' optimism is a result of analysts' reactions to management's expectations. Moreover, Abarbanell and Lehavy (2003) conclude that the conflicting evidence in prior research, regarding the existence and nature of analysts' biases and inefficiencies, is due to the reporting choices of firms. Abarbanell and Lehavy (2003) find an association between firms' recognition of unexpected accruals and the presence of the two asymmetries in distributions of forecast errors.

SOX 2002: Section 407

SOX 2002, section 407, focuses on the disclosure of the designated financial expertise in 10-K fillings, otherwise the firm must disclose if there is no designated financial expertise and why. The final regulation implementing Section 407 defines the audit committee financial expert as an individual with understanding of financial reporting and related internal controls, but not necessarily with direct experience in that function. This SEC rule expands the set of allowed qualifications to include two additional categories: persons with experience supervising the financial function (e.g., CEOs, Board chairs), and those with experience using financial information (e.g., venture capitalists, financial analysts). While "supervisory" and "user" expertise also relate to financial reporting, their experience is less directly tied to the preparation of financial reports. A proposed study in this domain is to investigate the association between different types of financial expertise and analysts' forecast optimism.

SOX 2002, Section 407 requires disclosure of the audit committee members that the company designates as "financial experts." At least one qualified individual on the audit committee must be designated (i.e., named in the10-K) as a financial expert. There are a number of motivations for testing the effect of SOX 2002, Section 407 on analysts' optimism. First, researchers are documenting more optimistic analysts' forecasts than pessimistic forecasts (Butler, 1991; Richardson, Teoh, and Wysocki, 2004; and Easterwood and Nutt, 1999). Second, a number of studies focus on the association between analysts' forecasts accuracy/error and corporate governance but none has tested the effect of SOX 2002, Section 407 (if any) on reducing analysts' forecasting errors. Prior research argues that analysts can play an important role in reducing the agency costs associated with misalignment of the interests between management/agent and shareholders/principles. If analysts provide earnings forecasts that are more informative, management of firms will be motivated to reward or beat those analysts' forecasts. In so doing, analysts can be a catalyst in reducing agency costs and in helping to discipline the market by punishing misbehaving managers and rewarding value creation.

Research on the association between analysts' forecasts and corporate governance might help enhance our understanding of corporate governance mechanisms (e.g., as the financial expert on the audit committee and would that help reduce forecast errors). Research in such areas also expands the literature that primarily focuses on board diligence, composition, and independence as the most effective governance tool in affecting the firm value, performance, and analyst's errors. For example, McKnight and Weir (2005) test the effect of audits, remuneration, and nomination committees on analysts' forecast errors and the dispersion of the errors. They find that the existence of these governance variables curbs earnings management, which in turn reduces the errors in analysts' forecasts. Likewise, Igan and Pinheiro (2004) document lower analysts' forecast optimism whenever there is aggressive earnings management. Bhat, Hope, and Kang (2006) examine the association between corporate governance transparency across 21 countries and analysts' forecast accuracy. They find that governance transparency affects analysts accuracy after controlling for financial transparency. Moreover, Knyazeva (2007) find an endogeneity effect between corporate governance and analysts' forecasts on firm value. In general, the main question is whether the existence of different types of financial expertise on the audit committee, especially the existence of a financial analyst as a 'user', has succeeded in reducing analysts' forecast optimism.

Corporate Governance and Analysts' Forecast Errors

A potentially important role of corporate governance is to reduce the errors and/or optimism in analysts' forecasts. That is, when financial analysts' earnings forecasts are more accurate they help reduce the information asymmetry between actual and forecasted earnings numbers. Using structural equation modeling, Aerts, Cormier, and Magnan (2007) find significant interrelationships between financial analysts' activities and corporate disclosure transparency for North American firms. They question how institutional governance affects financial analysts' behavior with regard to web-based performance disclosure. They suggest that corporate governance reduces the dispersion among analysts or analysts' earnings forecasts errors. Nowland (2008) investigates the effect of national governance codes on analysts' earnings forecasts. He tested this relationship on two levels – the company level and across companies (cross-sectional analysis) and finds that corporate governance codes in East Asia are associated with lower forecasting error. Although this study was based on voluntary corporate governance codes, the author concludes that voluntary governance systems are effective and influence the disclosure practices and analysts' forecasting errors.

Table 6. Corporate Governance and Firm Voluntary Disclosure

Study	Sample	Corporate Governance Measures	Control Variables	Firm Value Measures	Findings
Nowland (2008)	755 firms from Hong Kong, Indonesia, Malaysia, Philippines, Singapore, South Korea, Taiwan, and Thailand: 1993-2005	Company and national corporate governance codes	Number of analysts, size, growth, risk, earnings surprise, firm age, proportion of independent directors on the board	Analyst earnings forecasts	Corporate governance codes in East Asian associated with lower forecasting error
Aerts, Cormier, and Magnan (2007)	267 continental European Firms: 2002	Institutional governance	Endogeneity, industry, country effect, firm size, market to book value, media exposure	Web-based performance disclosure	Significant interrelationships between financial analysts' activities and corporate disclosure transparency
Lim, Matolcsy, and Chow (2007)	181 Australian firms: 2001	Board composition and independence	Firm size, leverage, Return on Assets, auditor, industry, top 20-shareholders, price-to-book ratio, management compensation	Voluntary disclosure index	Positive association between board composition and voluntary disclosure
Ajinkya, Bhojrai, and Sengupta (2005)	2934 annual forecasts: 1997-2002	Institutional ownership and board of directors' composition	Reg FD, standard deviation of analysts' forecasts, market value, auditor firm, litigation risk, loss firms	Properties of management earnings forecasts	Corporate governance has a favorable effect in terms of reducing managements' forecast errors

Table 6. Corporate Governance and Firm Voluntary Disclosure (cont.)

Study	Sample	Corporate Governance Measures	Control Variables	Firm Value Measures	Findings
Karamanou and Vefeas (2005)	275 firms: 1995-2000	Corporate board and audit committees	Information environment using analysts following, firm size dispersion in analysts' forecasts, high tech industry	voluntary financial disclosure practices (management earnings forecasts)	Firms with more effective board and audit committee structures are more likely to make or update earnings forecasts; effective corporate governance is associated with higher financial disclosure quality
Clement, Reese, and Swanson (2003)	384,112 firm years in US and ten countries: 2001	Cultural and corporate governance codes	frequency of issuing forecasts during year, portfolio complexity, days from issuance of forecast to fiscal year-end	Forecast accuracy among countries	Cultural and corporate governance influences the forecast accuracy among countries

Related, McKnight and Weir (2005) find that the independence of corporate governance sub-committees such as the audit committee, the nominating committee, and the remunerating committee reduce analysts' forecast errors and the dispersion of the errors. Clement, Reese, and Swanson (2003) divide ten countries into groups of similar cultural characteristics and argue that each group's analysts' forecasts differ based on the characteristics of financial analysts who are able to provide more accurate earnings forecasts than their peers. Overall, they find that cultural characteristics and corporate governance influences the forecast accuracy among countries. They also conclude that the forecasting error is affected by the years of experience, size frequency of forecast issuance across different countries, and the type of culture and corporate governance of the country. Based on the prior literature on both analysts' earnings forecasts and corporate governance, one would conjecture that financial analysts, as a financial expert on an audit committee, would be useful to a firm and might help reduce agency costs.

REFERENCES

Abarbanell, J. and Lehavy, R. 2003. Biased forecasts or biased earnings? The role of reported earnings in explaining apparent bias and over/under reaction in analysts' earnings forecasts. *Journal of Accounting and Economics* 36: 105-146.

Aerts, W., Cormier, D., and Magnan, M. 2007. The association between web-based corporate performance disclosure and financial analyst behaviour under different governance regimes. *Corporate Governance: An International Review* 15 (6): 1301-1328.

Ajinkya, B., Bhojraj, S., and Sengupta, P. 2005. The association between outside directors, institutional investors and the properties of management earnings forecasts. *Journal of Accounting Research* 43 (3): 343-376.

Bhat, G., Hope, O., and Kang, T. 2006. Does corporate governance transparency affect the accuracy of analyst forecasts? *Accounting and Finance* 46 (5): 715-732.

Brown, L. 1996. Analyst forecasting errors and their implications for security analysis: An alternative perspective. *Financial Analysts Journal* 52 (1): 40-47.

Butler, K., and Lang, L. 1991. The forecast accuracy of individual analysts: Evidence of forecast optimism. *The Accounting Review*, 81 (2): 377–397.

Chang, J., Cho, Y., and Shin, H. 2007. The change in corporate transparency of Korean firms after the Asian financial crisis: an analysis using analysts' forecast data. *Corporate Governance: An International Review* 15 (6): 1144-1167.

Clement, M., Reese, L., and Swanson, E. 2003. The influence of culture and corporate governance on the characteristics that distinguish superior analysts. *Journal of Accounting, Auditing, and Finance* 18 (4): 593-618.

Cowen, A., Groysbery, B., and Healy, P. 2006. Which types of analyst firms are more optimistic? *Journal of Accounting and Economics* 41 (1-2): 119-146.

Dreman, D. and Berry, M. 1995. Analyst forecasting errors and their implications for security analysis. *Financial Analysts Journal* 51 (3): 30-41.

Easterwood, J. and Nutt, S. 1999. Inefficiency in analysts' earnings forecasts: Systematic misreaction or systematic optimism? *The Journal of Finance* 54 (5): 1777-1797.

Healy, P., and Palepu, K. 2001. A review of the empirical disclosure literature. *Journal of Accounting and Economics* 31: 405–440.

Igan, D. and Pinheiro, M. 2004. Ownership structure and analysts' dorecasts. Working paper available at SSRN: http://ssrn.com/abstract=640721

Kadous, K., Krische, S., and Sedor, L. 2006. Using counter-explanation to limit analysts' forecast optimism. *The Accounting Review* 81 (2): 377-397.

Karamanou, I. and Vafeas, N. 2005. The association between corporate boards, audit committees, and management earnings forecasts: An Empirical Analysis. *Journal of Accounting Research* 43 (3): 453-486.

Knyazeva, D. 2007. Corporate governance, analyst following, and firm behavior. Working paper available at: http://www.simon.rochester.edu/fac/barclay/seminars/Diana%20Knyazeva_Job%20market%20paper_January%20draft.pdf

Lim, S., Matolcsy, Z., and Chow, D. 2007. The association between board composition and different types of voluntary disclosure. *European Accounting Review* 16 (3): 555–83.

Matsumoto, D. 2002. Management's incentives to avoid negative earnings surprises. *The Accounting Review* 77 (3): 483-514.

McKnight, P. and Weir, C. 2005. Corporate governance mechanisms and financial analysts forecasts. *Working paper* available at SSRN: http://ssrn.com/abstract=847484

Nowland, J. 2008. The effect of national governance codes on firm disclosure practices: evidence from analyst earnings forecasts. *Corporate Governance: An International Review* 16 (6): 475-491.

Richardson, S., Teoh, S., and Wysocki, P. 2004. The walk-down to Beatable Analyst Forecasts: The Role of Equity Issuance and Insider Trading Incentives. *Contemporary Accounting Research* 21 (4): 885-924.

Sedor, L. 2002. An explanation for unintentional optimism in analysts' earnings forecasts. *The Accounting Review* 77 (4): 731-753.

Skinner, D. 1994. Why firms voluntarily disclose bad news. *Journal of Accounting Research* 32: 38-61.

Chapter 9

CORPORATE GOVERNANCE AND AUDIT QUALITY

One major consequence of the accounting scandals by the beginning of the 21st century and consequently the passage of SOX 2002 is that quality auditing matters. A major consequence of SOX 2002 is the focus on the existence of an independent audit committee, which is hired by the board of directors of a firm. Audit committees have been the center of research on the association between corporate governance and financial reporting quality. In this chapter, we review the literature on the association between the auditing profession, including audit committees, audit fees, audit composition, audit quality (as a proxy for corporate governance) and financial reporting quality. The main focus of this review is post-SOX 2002.

AUDITING PROFESSION POST-SOX 2002

Research on the association between auditing processes and financial reporting quality focuses on audit committee compositions, qualifications, financial expertise (i.e., who is the designated financial expert), audit committee size, and number of meetings. SOX 2002 imposed stricter rules over the audit committee. First, all firms must have an audit committee that is composed either mostly or entirely of independent individuals. Second, the firm must mention whether the audit committee contains financial experts. Additionally, SOX 2002, Section 407 mandates disclosure of the designated financial experts on the audit committee in the firm's 10K filings. Third, this audit committee is responsible for the appointment of an external auditor for the firm. Prior research reports mixed results as to whether the independence of audit committee members is effective in monitoring the firm's financial statements. However, SOX 2002 mandates the de-listing of companies with less than 100 percent independent audit committee members. In studying the effect of SOX 2002 on auditing, DeFond and Francis (2005) argue that SOX 2002 broke down the auditing profession, increased audit fees by 50-100 percent, banned non-audit services performed by the incumbent auditor, made severe changes to auditing, and changed the auditing profession from a self-regulated industry to an industry that is now regulated by a quasi-governmental agency, the Public Company Accounting Oversight Board (PCAOB). Although there are no theories that explain the existence of audit committees, practice-related sources suggest that an audit committee plays a major role in overseeing the financial reporting process with the objective of securing high quality financial reporting. The following studies are examples of prior research on SOX 2002, auditing, and audit committees over the last three years as a major trend of research with a great deal of importance. The characteristics of the audit committee, especially the financial expertise of the audit committee, are a debatable topic that has increased in prominence in the last ten years. The SEC defines "audit committee financial expert" as:

> "An individual with understanding of financial reporting and related internal controls, but not necessarily with direct experience in that function."

SOX 2002, Section 407 expands the set of acceptable qualifications to define the term "financial expertise" to include two additional categories: persons with experience supervising the financial function (e.g., CEOs, board chairs), and those with experience using financial information (e.g., venture capitalists, financial analysts). While "supervisory" and "user" expertise also relate to financial reporting, such experience is less directly tied to the preparation of financial reports and might govern the way these financial statements are prepared. Although the SEC broadened the definition of financial expertise with respect to audit committee members, we did not find empirical evidence on the association between the broadened definition of audit committee members (as a new governance tool) and various aspects of firm value and performance. Therefore, we encourage researchers to explore this gap in the literature.

CORPORATE GOVERNANCE AND AUDIT QUALITY: GOVERNANCE MATTERS

The impact of SOX 2002 to publicly traded firms and investors is still a controversial issue. The auditing profession post-SOX 2002 has been a concern for lawmakers based on its direct effect on financial reporting quality, as well as its impact on the detection and prevention of corporate fraud. Cohen, Gaynor, and Krishnamoorthy, and Wright (2007) review literature on auditor communications with audit committees and boards of directors, with an emphasis on how such communications might affect financial reporting quality, internal control, and the auditor's performance. These authors argue that SOX 2002 increased the responsibility of audit committees and required an expanded dialogue between the external auditor and the audit committee. Although the literature related to the communication of internal controls and material weaknesses between the auditor and the audit committee is scarce, studies to date (e.g., Ashbaugh-Skaife et al. 2007) suggest some characteristics that must be considered when evaluating the risk of these weaknesses.

Similarly, Abbott, Parker, Peters, and Rama (2007) report that audit committees under SOX 2002 effectively monitor sourcing of a firm's total audit process because SOX 2002 restricts outsourcing of any internal audit functions to a firm's external auditor. Cohen, Gaynor, Krishnamoorthy, and Wright (2007) find that auditors' assessments of control risk are lower when the board is focused on monitoring the financial reporting process. This result suggests that the monitoring focus of the board (defined in terms of corporate governance measures such as independence of board members, diligence, etc.) may be associated with the quality of controls in an organization. Likewise, Bédard, Chtourou, and Courteau (2004) find that the presence of at least one member with financial expertise is associated with a lower likelihood of aggressive earnings management. Further, Cohen et al. (2007) find that audit committees with financial expertise and independent members are less likely to be associated with internal control problems.

Krishnan and Visvanathan (2007) examine the profile of audit committees and auditors (such as auditor size, auditor changes, and auditor tenure) for firms that reported internal control material weakness after the passage of SOX 2002, Section 404 (after December 2004). They find that firms reporting weaknesses in their internal control systems were characterized by prior restatement of financial statements, a higher number of meetings of the audit committee, lower proportion of financial experts on the audit committee, and more auditor changes. Krishnan and Visvanathan (2007) use a sample of homogenous firms in terms of complexity of operations, profitability, and growth; however, their sample was very small. They examined the audit committee activity rather than its composition and recommended future research to examine attributes of governance other than size of audit committee or the number of independent directors, since changes brought about by SOX 2002 essentially create uniformity in these variables.

DeFond, Hann, and Hu, (2005) study the effect of audit committee independence on stock returns pre-SOX 2002, using 702 firms with newly appointed outside directors assigned to audit committees. They use three-day cumulative abnormal returns as the returns window around the announcement of those 702 newly appointed outside directors. Moreover, they test the market reaction to the appointment of outside directors with financial expertise on the audit committee to inquiry the effect of SOX 2002 on the stock market. They find a positive market reaction to the appointment of outside directors with financial expertise assigned to the audit committees. This reaction was robust for firms with strong corporate governance structure and they conclude that financial expertise on an audit committee helps enhance shareholder value.

Patterson and Smith (2007) investigate the effect of SOX 2002 on auditing intensity and internal control strength. More specifically, they investigate how SOX 2002 affected the expected fraud, audit risk, and expected undetected fraud. They find that SOX 2002 increased the internal control strength and decreased the amount of fraud. However, the amount of internal control testing can either increase or decrease. The chances for internal control testing to decrease are high because as control strength increases, control testing provides less information about the probability of fraud.

Braswell and Mauldin (2004) examine the work experience and background of audit committee members' financial expertise pre- and post-SOX 2002, Section 407 using a sample of 195 firms. They find that firms complied with the pre-requirement of the SEC listing by using financial expertise in 2001. Also, they find that firms increased accounting expertise on the audit committee starting from 2003 relative to prior years (post-SOX 2002, Section 407.) They classify each audit committee member into one of four groups: accounting expert, CEO/President, finance expert, or other. They argue that the percent of firms with at least one accounting expert increased from 45 percent in 2001 to 49 percent in 2002 and to 64 percent in 2003 and this increase is statistically significant. They suggest that the increase in the number of audit committee members with financial expertise is consistent with agency theory and the usefulness of SOX 2002 to the firm in aligning managers' interests with shareholders' interests. They find that almost 36 percent of firms do not have an accounting expert on their audit committee and about 80 percent of firms have at least one CEO/President with no direct accounting or finance experience on their audit committee. In the same vein, Krishnan and Ye (2005) suggest that financial expertise and audit committees offer positive monitoring effects and resulted in an increased likelihood that shareholders would ratify the audit selection. Krishnan and Ye (2005) also document that financial expertise and audit committees increased the confidence in management choices. Moreover, Krishnan (2005) argues that independent audit committees and audit committees with financial expertise are highly associated with less likelihood of internal control problems.

CORPORATE GOVERNANCE AND AUDIT QUALITY: GOVERNANCE DOES NOT MATTER

DeFond and Francis (2005) claim that the number of audit failures after SOX 2002 has declined and even reached an annual failure rate that approaches zero. Raghunandan and Rama (2006) examine the association between audit fees and internal control disclosures made post-SOX 2002, Section 404. They used a sample of 660 manufacturing firms with a December 31, 2004 fiscal year-end that had filed their Section 404 reports by May 15, 2005. The authors find that the mean (median) audit fees for the sample firms post-SOX 2002 is 86 (128) percent higher than the corresponding fees for pre-SOX 2002. Also, audit fees for 2004 are 43 percent higher for firms with a material weakness disclosure compared to firms without a material weakness disclosure. Audit fees for 2003 are not associated with an internal control material weakness disclosure. They also report that the association between audit fees and the presence of a material weakness disclosure is not dependent on the type of material weakness (systemic or non-systemic).

Ettredge, Li and Scholz (2007) investigate the relationship between higher audit fees (both levels and changes) and auditor's dismissals post-SOX 2002. They find that clients paying higher fees are more likely to dismiss auditors. Also, the dismissals are associated with companies with material weakness, small companies, and companies with going-concern reports. They find that post-SOX 2002 the majority of Big 4 clients who dismiss their auditors hire non-Big 4 auditors. However, their results might be influenced by a "sample period bias" since they analyzed the audit of the first full fiscal year subsequent to SOX 2002. Related, Ettredge, Li, and Sun (2006) find that the existence of a material weakness in internal control over financial statements is associated with significantly longer auditor delays. They also find that the type of material weakness affects the length of audit delay. General/firm-wide material weaknesses are associated with longer delays than account/specific material weaknesses. Moreover, material weaknesses associated with certain control problems (e.g., personnel, process, segregation of duties, and closing process) result in even more audit delays. Overall, they hypothesized that companies that implement the new internal control over financial reporting requirements experience increased audit delay and, as a result, risk jeopardizing investor's confidence in their financial statements. These results support the notion that SOX 2002, Section 404 assessment of internal control is in conflict with the SEC demand to shorten 10-K filing deadlines. Ettredge et al. (2006) used all firms that file Section 404 reports from January 2005 to June 2005.

According to DeFond and Francis (2005), SOX 2002 triggered two engagement-specific characteristics: auditor tenure and the revolving door policy. SOX 2002 initiated the argument that long auditor tenure may create a self-serving bias and reduce audit quality. Likewise, short auditor tenure may lower audit quality due to a learning curve concept. Therefore, DeFond and Francis (2005) advocate for "auditor retention" instead of an auditor tenure concept introduced by SOX 2002. Under the revolving door policy, accounting firm alumni take positions at clients, although SOX 2002 mandated a one year waiting period for audit employees who left an accounting firm to be an executive for a former client firm.

To sum up, results on the importance of auditing, audit committees, audit quality, and audit fees post-SOX 2002 are inconclusive. Church, Davis, and McCracken (2008) suggest that future research should be directed towards studying whether auditors have a greater influence over the financial reporting process post-SOX 2002. In other words, does SOX 2002 help auditors' negotiating position to resolve disagreements with the client (based on increased role of audit committee)? In general, audit committee members should be able to fully face challenges related to the nature and type of various control weaknesses. Further, Cohen, Gaynor, Krishnamoorthy, and Wright (2007) suggest that future research should focus on whether audit committees with industry and financial expertise are better able to understand the nature and type of control weaknesses (relative to those committees without such expertise) and be able to communicate with management and the auditor to assure a strong system of internal controls.

Table 7. Corporate Governance and Audit Quality

Study	Sample	Corporate Governance Measures	Control Variables	Firm Value Measures	Findings
Abbott, Parker, Peters and Rama (2007)	88 firms: January 1991 - December 1999	Audit committee under SOX 2002	Oversight mechanisms, management incentives and management characteristics	Firm's total audit process	Audit committee under SOX 2002 is effectively monitoring sourcing of firm's total audit process because SOX 2002 restricts outsourcing of any internal audit (IA) functions to firms' external auditors
Cohen, Gaynor, Krishnamoorthy and Wright (2007)	Survey of available research	Auditor communications with audit committees and board of directors	None	Financial reporting quality, internal control, auditor's performance	SOX 2002 increased responsibly of audit committee, requires expanded dialogue between external auditor and audit committee
Ettredge, Li and Scholz (2007)	428 firms: 2003	Audit fees (both levels and changes)	Client size, financial condition, growth, auditor industry specialization	Auditor's dismissals post SOX 2002	Clients paying higher fees are more likely to dismiss auditors; dismissals are associated with companies with material weaknesses, small companies, and companies with going-concern reports; post-SOX 2002, the majority of Big 4 clients who dismiss their auditors hire non-Big 4 auditors; results might have sample period bias since they analyze audit of first full fiscal year subsequent to SOX 2002
Krishnan and Visvanathan (2007)	118 firms: 2004-2005	Audit committees, auditors	Profitability, complexity, growth, organizational changes	Internal control deficiencies	More meetings of audit committee, lower proportion of 'financial experts' on audit committee, and more auditor changes characterize firms that report weaknesses in internal controls compared to firms with no weaknesses

Table 7. Corporate Governance and Audit Quality (cont.)

Study	Sample	Corporate Governance Measures	Control Variables	Firm Value Measures	Findings
Patterson and Smith (2007)	Theoretical framework	SOX 2002	None	Expected fraud, audit risk, strength of internal control, expected undetected fraud	SOX 2002 increased internal control strength and decreased amount of fraud; the amount of internal control testing can either increase or decrease. Chances for internal control testing to decrease are high because as control strength increases, control testing provides less information about probability of fraud
Ettredge, Li, and Sun (2006)	2,344 firms: 2003 Matched sample: 2004	Existence of a material weakness in internal control	Client size, industry, financial condition, extraordinary items, business complexity, net losses, restatements of financial reports, audit fees, auditors' opinions on financial statements, auditor change	Auditor delays	SOX 2002 section 404 assessment of internal control is in conflict with SEC demand to shorten 10-K filing deadlines
Raghunandan and Rama (2006)	660 firms: 2003-2005	Audit fees	Client size, complexity, risk	Internal control disclosures	Mean (median) audit fees for sample firms post-SOX 2002 (2004) is 86 (128) percent higher than corresponding fees for pre-SOX 2002 (2003); audit fees for 2004 are 43 percent higher for firms with a material weakness disclosure compared to firms without material weakness disclosure; audit fees for 2003 are not associated with an internal control material weakness disclosure

Table 7. Corporate Governance and Audit Quality (cont.)

Study	Sample	Corporate Governance Measures	Control Variables	Firm Value Measures	Findings
Defond, Hann and Hu (2005)	702 firms: 2002-2003	Audit committee independence, financial expertise	Firm size, market-to-book	Stock returns	Positive market reaction to appointment of outside directors with financial expertise on audit committees; reaction was stronger for firms with strong corporate governance structure; financial expertise on audit committee helps enhance shareholder value
Krishnan and Ye (2005)	383 firms: 2001	Independent audit committee, audit committee with financial expertise	Auditor's total fees, industry effect	Likelihood of internal control problems	Independent audit committee and audit committee with financial expertise highly associated with less likelihood of internal control problems
Bédard, Chtourou, and Courteau (2004)	200 firms: 1996	Audit committee with at least one member with financial expertise, audit committee independence, activities	Earnings, cash flow, size, Return on Assets	Aggressive earnings management	Presence of at least one member with financial expertise is associated with a lower likelihood of aggressive earnings management
Braswell and Mauldin (2004)	195 firms: 2002-2004	SOX 2002, Section 407	Firm size, industry	Work experience and background of audit committee members	Firms increased accounting expertise on audit committee starting from 2003 relative to prior years

References

Abbott, L., Parker, S., Peters, G., and Rama, D. 2007. Corporate governance, audit quality, and the Sarbanes-Oxley Act: Evidence from internal audit outsourcing. *The Accounting Review* 82 (4): 803-835.

Ashbaugh-Skaife, H., Collins, D., and Kinney, W. 2007. The discovery and reporting of internal control deficiencies prior to SOX 2002-mandated audits. *Journal of Accounting and Economics* 44: 166-192.

Bédard, J., Chtourou, S., and Courteau, L. 2004. The Effect of audit committee expertise, independence, and activity on aggressive earnings management. *Auditing: A Journal of Practice & Theory* 23 (2): 13-35.

Braswell, M. and Mauldin, E. 2004. Changes in Audit Committee Financial Expertise. *Working paper.*

Church, B., Davis, S., and McCracken, S. 2008. The auditor's reporting model: A literature overview and research synthesis. *Accounting Horizons* 22 (1): 69–90.

Cohen, J., Gaynor, L., Krishnamoorthy, G., and Wright, A. 2007. Auditor communications with the audit committee and the board of directors: Policy recommendations and opportunities for future research. *Accounting Horizons* 21 (2): 165–187.

DeFond, M. and Francis, J. 2005. Audit Research after Sarbanes-Oxley. *Auditing: A Journal of Practice and Theory* 24: 5-30.

DeFond, M., Hann, R., and Hu, X. 2005. Does the market value financial expertise on audit committees of boards of directors? *Journal of Accounting Research* 43: 153-193.

Ettredge, M., Li, C., and Scholz, S. 2007. Audit fees and auditor dismissals in the Sarbanes-Oxley era. *Accounting Horizons* 21 (4): 371–386.

______ , ______ , and Sun, L. 2006. The impact of SOX 2002 Section 404 internal control quality assessment on audit delay in the SOX 2002 era. *Auditing: A Journal of Practice & Theory* 25 (2): 1-23.

Krishnan, G. and Visvanathan, G. 2007. Reporting internal control deficiencies in the post-Sarbanes-Oxley era: The role of auditors and corporate governance. *International Journal of Auditing* 11: 73-90.

Krishnan, J. 2005. Audit committee quality and internal control: An empirical analysis. *The Accounting Review* 80 (2): 649-675.

______ and Ye, Z. 2005. Why some companies seek shareholder ratification on auditor selection. *Accounting Horizons* 19 (4): 237-254.

Patterson E. and Smith, J. 2007. The effects of Sarbanes-Oxley on auditing and internal control strength. *The Accounting Review* 82 (2): 427-455.

Raghunandan, K. and Rama, D. 2006. SOX Section 404 material weakness disclosures and audit fees. *Auditing: A Journal of Practice & Theory* 25 (1): 99-114.

PART IV.
CORPORATE GOVERNANCE AND INTERNATIONAL STUDIES

Chapter 10

CORPORATE GOVERNANCE AND THE FIRM: INTERNATIONAL EVIDENCE

In parts two and three of this book, our analysis of corporate governance codes focuses on U.S. firm performance and reporting quality. We believe it is equally important to discuss some of the research relating to corporate governance codes for non-U.S. firms. Therefore, this chapter provides a review of a sample of international research on the usefulness of corporate governance codes to international firms. As the empirical evidence shows, results are again inconclusive on the international level on whether corporate governance adds value to international firms.

CORPORATE GOVERNANCE IN INTERNATIONAL FIRMS: IS IT DIFFERENT?

Corporate governance, in the international context, is a recent debatable topic such as the situation in the U.S. For example, the China Securities Regulatory Commission mandates issuance of quarterly financial reports starting in 2002. Accordingly, McGunagle (2007) investigates the changes and the effect of business reforms (the role of board of directors and financial reporting) on corporate governance in China. Results indicate that the Asian crisis prompted the implementation of governance mechanisms that include the existence of independent directors and audit committees in the companies listed on the stock exchanges; however, in Asia, the number of qualified independent directors is limited. Also, the new corporate governance in Asia is similar to that of the Anglo-American “shareholder” model. Overall, results suggest that while China made major reforms to strengthen its corporate governance after the Asian crisis in the 1990’s, much work is still required to achieve an effective governance system.

Corporate governance in non-U.S. firms could differ from those in U.S. firms. Cornelius’s (2005) surveys the quality of governance practices in a large sample of emerging markets and the effect of corporate governance quality on the perceived weakness in the institutional framework in which these international firms operate. Results suggest that corporate governance practices are weaker in emerging markets than those in developed economies. Also, legal institutions are instrumental for corporate governance; however, politics, cultural, and historical roots play a major role. Some emerging markets have made significant progress toward reducing the quality gap between corporate governance practices and their perceived weakness in their institutional framework. A significant implication of this study is that good governance practices at the company level may not be constrained by its country governance environment. In reviewing the international evidence on the usefulness of corporate governance, we categorize research into two main streams: (1) corporate governance and firm performance; and (2) corporate governance and financial reporting quality.

Corporate Governance and Investor Protection

A number of the studies in this section analyze the association between corporate governance, legal protections, and investors, especially large shareholders. In general, large shareholders have a substantial investment in the company and have voting power. As a result, these shareholders are likely to mitigate the collective action problem among dispersed shareholders, to engage in rational investing, and to be more committed to the firm in the long term. Evidence from these studies suggests that good (strong) corporate governance increases investors’ protection. Future research might be directed towards studying the effect (interplay) of corporate governance, legal protections, and investors in developing versus emerging economies. In addition, more research on the impact of shareholder activism in developed, developing, and emerging economies could help inform appropriate corporate governance mechanisms to protect shareholders (large and small) and also enhance firm performance.

Dargenidou, McLeay, and Raonic (2007) investigate the interactive effect of corporate ownership, corporate governance, and investor protection on the incorporation of current value shocks in the accounting earnings of European companies. The sample consists of 11,769 firm-year observations from 1988-2002 for firms in Belgium, Denmark, Finland, France, Germany, Italy, Netherlands, Norway, Spain, Sweden and the UK. Results indicate that accounting behavior is a function of the demand created by shareholders. Also, rigid corporate governance practices in Europe can substitute for weaknesses in investor protection provisions in law. When investor protection is weak and corporate governance does not separate supervision from management, the findings showed a systematic understatement in the recognition of bad news. This could be interpreted as insiders (such as controlling shareholders and managers) concealing the effect of unfavorable information on current and short term earnings expectations. Results show that effective investor protection legislation and well-defined monitoring structures are able to compensate for these adverse effects of insider control. Results also suggest that corporate governance practices substitute for the lack of investor protection and vice versa.

In the same line of research, DeFond and Hung (2004) test whether the measures of good corporate governance, offered by laws and enforced by legal institutions that protect investors, are associated with an important role of good corporate governance (i.e., identifying and terminating poorly performing CEOs). In other words, the authors investigate the effect of investor protection on the association between CEO turnover and firm performance in the turnover decision. The authors use stock returns and earnings to assess CEO performance. The initial sample consists of countries with (1) at least 100 companies in the last year of the Worldscope database, and (2) the necessary data to compute each of the country-level variables. The final sample consisted of 21,483 firm-year observations in 33 countries. Results indicate that strong law enforcement institutions significantly improve the association between CEO turnover and poor performance, whereas extensive investor protection laws do not. Also, countries with strong law enforcement have a CEO turnover that is more likely to be associated with poor stock returns when stock prices are more informative. The authors claim that the set of laws they examined may not be the set that are most important in promoting good governance. Empirical results of prior research show that countries with developed corporate governance offer strong investor protection. This result might be due to the fact that investor protection fosters good corporate governance that in turn instills investor confidence.

Similarly, Sarker and Sarker (2000) explore the role of large shareholders in monitoring company value of firms in a developing and emerging economy (India). In India, the corporate governance system is a hybrid of outsider-dominated market-based systems of the UK and the U.S., and the insider-dominated market-based systems of Germany and Japan. The authors find that blockholdings by directors increase company value after a certain level of holdings, but there was no evidence that institutional investors are active in governance. Large shareholders have substantial investments and voting power, are likely to mitigate the problem present among dispersed shareholders, are likely to engage in relational investing, and are likely to be more committed to the firm in the long term. Developing countries rely more on banks and equity markets to finance long-term projects than do developed countries. The authors find the relationship between shareholding and company value to be positive and statistically significant. These results suggest that other blockholders may have a positive role in mitigating agency problems in the presence of legal protection.

Corporate Governance and Firm Performance

Stock Price Performance

De Medeiros and Da Silveira (2007) study the relationship between corporate values and stock performance from the beginning of 2003 to the end of 2005 in 16 banks of six Latin American countries (Argentina, Brazil, Chile, Colombia, Peru, and Mexico). The authors use ethics, corporate governance, social responsibility, sustainability, and transparency as measures of corporate values. They use stock volatility, liquidity, and abnormal stock returns to measure stock performance. The authors test whether the corporate values are instrumental to stock performance in terms of reducing volatility and its associated risk and hence the cost of capital. Results indicate a negative and significant relationship between corporate governance values and liquidity and volatility, as expected. A possible explanation for the reported negative significant relationship is that higher corporate governance values reduce the possibility of speculation and arbitrage and this lowers stock volatility, risk associated with this volatility, and abnormal stock returns. Moreover, the authors suggest that higher corporate values increase investors' confidence in the stocks, and hence, diminish trading of this stock in the short-term. This would lead to reduction in information asymmetry and speculation in the capital markets and would be beneficial for stability of long-term investment.

Likewise, Alexakis, Balios, Papagelis, and Xanthakis (2006) examine the behavior of stock returns after the enforcement of corporate governance legislation in Greece, using a sample of 30 stocks of Greek listed companies for the period 24 September 1999 to 11 February 2004 (divided into three time periods to examine volatility). Results indicate that volatility was reduced. The authors note that this might be the case due to the introduction of corporate governance; however, other factors might also have impacted volatility.

Bauer, Gunster, and Otten (2004) analyze whether good corporate governance leads to higher common stock returns and enhances firm value in Europe. The authors constructed portfolios consisting of well-governed and poorly-governed companies, and then compared the performance of the two portfolios for the period 1997-2002. To measure each company's quality of governance, the authors used the Deminor's corporate governance ratings (based on four criteria: rights and duties of shareholders, range of takeover defenses, disclosure on corporate governance, and board structure and functioning). The sample includes Euro zone companies in the FTSE Euro top 300 index. Results indicate that portfolios of companies with high corporate governance standards perform better than companies with lower corporate governance standards. The authors suggest that their results should convince institutional investors to account for corporate governance standards in their investment process. Overall, they find no evidence on the relationship between corporate governance and firm value.

Pajuste's (2002) introduces a comparative approach on the Central and Eastern European stock markets after the first decade of transition. Pajuste (2002) studies the importance of corporate governance issues (rule of law, enforcement, minority shareholder protection, etc.) in determining the level of stock market performance (stock returns and liquidity) in nine Central and Eastern European (CEE) countries over the period June 1994 – June 2001: the Czech Republic, Estonia, Hungary, Latvia, Lithuania, Poland, Romania, Slovakia and Slovenia. The results suggest that the CEE stock markets have lower returns and higher risk than those associated with developed markets. The evidence suggests that the enforcement of law matters more than the quality of law. Moreover, the protection of minority shareholders (legal index) has a significant impact on market activity, measured by market turnover to market capitalization ratio. Stock market activity, measured by equity turnover as a share of market capitalization, is significantly dependent on the level of minority shareholder protection (in laws).

Dahyaa, Lonie, and Power (2000) investigate whether share prices and operating profits are affected by boards' decisions to change the composition of their top management teams and whether the UK companies' earnings are manipulated by newly appointed, retiring, or departing managers. Both of these lines of inquiry are important issues for corporate governance. Dahyaa, Lonie, and Power (2000) find no share price response to the appointment or departure of senior executives. That is, price changes were insignificant.

Kang and Shivdasani (1996) investigate whether the Japanese governance system enhances shareholder wealth by examining stock-price effects of top management turnover for 432 Japanese corporations from 1985 to 1990. They find that these announcements are associated with significant positive abnormal returns, which are greater when turnover is forced relative to those when turnover represented a normal sequence. The evidence suggests that disciplinary decisions of Japanese governance mechanisms were consistent with shareholder wealth maximization. Japanese boards consist of two types of directors: inside directors that have been lifelong employees of the firm and outside directors who were former employees of other organizations and typically joined the firm as a corporate director. They also find that governance mechanisms were particularly active during outside succession. Although the Japanese governance mechanisms pursue objectives other than shareholder wealth maximization, the evidence of this study suggests that at least during top management turnover, pursuit of such objectives enhances shareholder wealth.

Firm Value

Ariff, Ibrahim and Othman (2007) investigate the influence of eight firm level characteristics on the Corporate Governance Reporting rating in Malaysia. The firms' corporate governance levels examined in this study were firm profitability, leverage, growth, market valuation, size, age, ownership structure, and countries of operation, using logit analysis. The sample was composed of 95 publicly listed companies based on the Corporate Governance Reporting Initiative, 2004. Results indicate that only firm size had a strong relation with corporate governance ratings.

Hsu (2007) examines the influence of corporate governance on firm values using a structural equation model and data from 258 companies listed on Taiwan's stock exchange in 2003. The corporate governance mechanisms examined are equity ownership structure, directors' and supervisors' structure, and information transparency. Results show that information transparency influences the efficiency of corporate governance (the equity ownership structure and directors' and supervisors' structure) and enhances firm values. Also, results confirm the validity of the structural model in this study and a strong association between the composition of board of directors and information transparency.

McIntyre, Murphy, and Mitchell (2007) investigate whether boards can play a major role in contributing to firm performance and effectiveness. The authors use data from 151 firms on the Canadian TSE 300 Composite Index for 2001. Specifically, this paper examines the relationship between key board composition variables and firm performance using cross-sectional regression analyses to examine the nature of the relationships between board composition and firm performance. Results show that the key board composition variables (high levels of experience, appropriate team size, moderate levels of variation in age and team tenure) are associated with firm performance.

The purpose of Ting (2006) was to examine when corporate governance adds value to a firm. The sample included 207 IPO companies listed in the Taiwan Security Exchange from 1992-2002. Two models were used to measure a firm's value: market-based performance (total returns) and accounting-based performance (EPS, ROA, and ROE). Management style was used as a proxy for an entrenchment effect and corporate governance. Results suggest that corporate governance mechanisms add value to the firm when executives realize its importance.

Shen, Hsu, and Chen (2006) examine the relationship between firm values and corporate governance using a sample of 67 companies for the years 1990-1992. The dependent variable in this study was the firm value (net present value per stock, stock price, and the book value per stock ratio) and the independent variables were: ownership ratio of the board of directors and supervisors, managerial ownership, institutional ownership ratio, and the ratio of the pledged stocks held by the board of directors and supervisors. Results suggest a significant positive relationship between ownership ratio of board of directors and book value per share. Institutional ownership ratios had no relationship with price earnings ratio.

Filatotchev, Lien, and Piesse (2005) investigate the effect of ownership structure and board characteristics on firm performance in the Taiwan market. They find that the presence of institutional ownership, foreign financial institution, and family ownership and control are associated with better firm performance using different proxies for firm performance after controlling for possible endogeneity. Firm performance proxies used in this study include accounting ratios, sales per issued capital, earnings per share, and market-to-book ratio. Filatotchev et al. (2005) also find that board independence is positively associated with positive financial performance. However, one thing to note is that board characteristics in Taiwan are significantly different than those in the U.S. or UK. In Taiwan, there are no board meetings and the focus is on individual characteristics rather than board characteristics as a whole.

The purpose of the study conducted by Filatotchev, Lien, and Piesse (2005) was to analyze the effects of ownership structure and board characteristics on performance of 228 large family owned but publicly traded firms listed on the Taiwan Stock Exchange (TSE). Results show that family control is not associated with performance measured in terms of accounting ratios, sales per issued capital, earnings per share, and market-to-book value. However, share ownership by institutional investors and foreign financial institutions is associated with better performance. Results also confirm that board independence from a founding family and board members' financial interests has a positive impact on performance. Overall, results suggest that the presence of an independent Chairman did not seem to affect performance.

Bauer, Gunster, and Otten (2004) analyze the relationship between corporate governance and firm performance, as approximated by Net-Profit-Margin (NPM) and Return-on-Equity (ROE). All firms were ranked on the basis of their corporate governance rating for the European Monetary Union (EMU) and the UK sample, respectively. For the EMU, the authors assign the 20 percent of companies with the highest corporate governance rating to the "Good Governance Portfolio" and the bottom 20 percent were allocated to the "Bad Governance Portfolio". While they find economically large excess returns to a zero-investment corporate governance strategy in the UK, the authors find no evidence of a relationship between governance and firm valuation. This result suggests that the UK market was still changing, but in the long-run, the excess returns to corporate governance should translate in a higher firm valuation for better governed firms. In the EMU, the authors find a stronger relationship between governance and firm value. This evidence might imply that current corporate governance standards have already been incorporated in stock prices. The reason investors in Eurozone companies account more for a firm's governance standards than UK investors could be explained by the fact that Eurozone countries traditionally tend to have poorer governance standards. Overall, they find no evidence of a relationship between corporate governance and firm value.

Drobetz, Schillhofer, and Zimmermann (2004) investigate whether differences in the quality of firm-level corporate governance helps to explain firm performance in a cross-section of companies within a single jurisdiction.

The authors use a sample of 91 German publicly-listed firms, and collect 30 governance proxies divided into 5 categories: corporate governance commitment, shareholder rights, transparency, management and supervisory board matters, and auditing. These governance proxies are derived from the recommendations set by the German Corporate Governance Code (GCGC). The results show that firms with better corporate governance are highly correlated with better operating performance, higher stock returns, and higher market valuation.

Drobetz, Schillhofer, and Zimmermann (2004) use five governance proxies derived from the recommendations set by the German Corporate Governance Code (GCGC) to investigate the association between these governance variables and firm performance in Germany. They find that firms with better corporate governance are highly correlated with better operating performance, higher stock returns, and higher market valuation. Likewise, Shen, Hsu, and Chen (2006) find a significant positive relationship between ownership ratio of board of directors and book value per share in Taiwan. Institutional ownership ratios had no relationship with price earnings ratio.

Judge, Naoumova and Koutzevol (2003) use a survey to study the relationship between CEO duality and firm performance in Russia. Their findings were in line with the main purpose of the 1996 Russian Federal law which prohibits CEO duality. Overall, they find a negative relationship between the 'informal' CEO duality and firm performance. Likewise, they find that the more firms aggressively apply retrenchment strategy, the more negative the relationship between insider directors and firm performance. Overall, Judge et al. (2003) suggest that an effective corporate governance structure is crucial to firm performance in Russia. However, Ezzamel and Watson (1997) investigate the separation between decision management/CEO and decision control/chairman in the UK and finds that this separation is associated with better corporate performance.

Hiraki, Hideaki, Ito, Kuroki, and Masuda (2003) examine the impact of alternative corporate governance mechanisms (main bank, intercorporate shareholding, managerial ownership) on firm value in Japan. The authors use panel data on equity ownership and bank loans of manufacturing companies listed on the Tokyo Stock Exchange for 1985-1998. They find that one-way ownership by banks was positively related to firm value; that one-way ownership by non-financial corporations was positively related to firm value; and that managerial ownership was monotonically and positively related to firm value.

Mitton (2002) analyzes firm-level differences in variables related to corporate governance and finds a strong impact on firm performance during the East Asian financial crisis of 1997 to 1998. The sample includes 398 firms from Indonesia, Korea, Malaysia, the Philippines, and Thailand. He finds that high stock price performance is associated with firms that have indicators of higher disclosure quality, with firms that have higher outside ownership concentration, and with firms that are focused rather than diversified. The results suggest that companies offering higher disclosure quality, greater transparency, a more favorable ownership structure, and a more focused organization appear to have provided greater protection to their minority shareholders during the financial crisis.

Volpin's (2002) study considers the determinants of executive turnover and firm valuation as a function of ownership and control structure. The sample for this study includes 205 Italian firms over the period 1986 to 1997 (1,611 observations). The results provide direct evidence on the performance of corporate governance in a country characterized by low legal protection for investors, firms with large controlling shareholders, and some separation of ownership. Specifically, governance improves when the controlling shareholder's objectives are more aligned with those of minority shareholders. Large minority shareholders do not appear to improve governance.

Corporate Governance and Financial Reporting Quality

Earnings Informativeness

Machuga and Teitel (2007) test whether the implementation of the Mexican Corporate Governance Code improved the earnings quality and increased investor confidence by providing more reliable and transparent financial reporting. They use a sample of 92 Mexican firms (January 200) and a variety of earnings quality characteristics that include: income smoothing, timely loss recognition, and abnormal accruals. Results indicate that management decreased the use of accruals to manipulate earnings after the implementation of Mexican Corporate Governance Code and therefore the quality of earnings improved after the adoption of the code.

Fan and Wong (2002) examine the association between earnings informativeness and the ownership structure of 977 companies in seven East

Asian economies. Earnings informativness in this study was measured by the returns-earnings relation. The authors argued that the Asian financial crisis forced the East Asian economies to re-examine the adequacy of their corporate financial reporting; however, despite efforts to improve transparency by imposing new accounting and disclosure rules, the perception is that the quality of financial reporting is still low. The authors find that high ownership concentration is associated with low earnings informativeness, and claimed that these results are generalizable to other parts of the world because the concentrated corporate ownership in East Asia is representative of corporate structures throughout the world (compared to diffuse corporate ownership in the U.S. and UK).

Earnings Management

Sánchez-Ballesta and García-Meca (2007) examine the relationship between ownership structure, discretionary accruals, and the informativeness of earnings for a sample of 64 Spanish non-financial companies listed on the Madrid Stock Exchange during the period 1999–2002. Results suggest a non-linear relationship between insider ownership and discretionary accruals and between insider ownership and earnings explanatory power for returns. This result suggests that insider ownership improves the informativeness of earnings and restrains earnings management when the proportion of shares held by insiders was not too high. However, when insiders own a large percentage of shares, the relationship between insider ownership, discretionary accruals, and earnings informativeness reverses.

Ding, Zhang, and Zhang (2007) research the effects of a firm's ownership structure on earnings management in the Chinese capital market. The authors measured ownership concentration and different ownership types (specifically the difference between the state as blockholders and private blockholders). The authors use a sample of 273 privately-owned and state-owned Chinese companies listed in 2002. Results showed that the relationship between earnings management measures and ownership concentration was a non-linear, inverted U-shape relationship known as the "entrenchment versus alignment" effect. This result indicated that the privately-owned listed companies tended to maximize their accounting earnings more than state-owned listed firms. However, the entrenchment effect of ownership concentration on earnings management was weaker in privately-owned firms than in state-owned firms. The results also confirm that firms use different methods to manipulate earnings, such as operating-related accrual mechanisms and non-operating transactions with related parties.

Jaggi and Tsui (2007) test the association between corporate governance and earnings management for a sample of 1,588 observations for Hong Kong firms over the period 1995-1999. They measured corporate governance by independent directors and earnings management by insider selling. Results support a positive association between earnings management and insider selling, which was especially evident before the 1997 Asian Financial Crisis. Results also suggest that executives manage earnings to maximize their private benefits from insider selling and that earnings management can be reduced by independent directors when no member of the family with majority ownership is present on corporate boards as a director.

Lai and Tam (2007) explore whether independent directors serve an effective role as a corporate governance mechanism in reducing income-smoothing earnings management in China. The authors use a sample of 2,634 firm-year observations for the years 2000-2002 to examine whether the adoption of independent directors affects the negative relationship between the change in cash flows and accruals. Their results suggest that Chinese firms that voluntarily adopt independent directors, as well as firms that have a larger fraction of independent directors, are more likely to reduce the practice of income smoothing.

Shen and Chih (2007) study the impact of corporate governance on earnings management using firm-level governance data. The authors also use financial ratios of nine Asian countries (Hong Kong, India, Indonesia, Korea, Malaysia, the Philippines, Singapore, Taiwan and Thailand) as well as the country-level governance data used in past studies. The sample included 495 companies from April 2001 to February 2002. Earnings management was measured by earnings smoothing and earnings aggressiveness. Results suggest that firms with good corporate governance tend to have less earnings management; large firms are more likely to smooth earnings, but good corporate governance mitigated this behavior. Firms with higher growth are more likely to engage in earnings smoothing and earnings aggressiveness, but good corporate governance mitigated this effect.

Table 8. Corporate Governance and the Firm: International Evidence

Study	Sample	Corporate Governance Measures	Control Variables	Firm Value Measures	Findings
Ariff, Ibrahim and Othman (2007)	95 firms: 2004	Profitability, leverage, growth, market valuation, size, age, ownership structure, countries of operation	Ownership structure, board characteristics, leverage	Corporate governance reporting rating in Malaysia	Only firm size had a strong relation with corporate governance ratings: suggests an endogenous corporate governance structure
Dargenidou, McLeay, and Raonic (2007)	11,769 firm-year observations: 1988-2002	Interactive effect of corporate ownership, corporate governance, investor protection	Extreme values	Current value of stocks	Accounting behavior is a function of demand created by shareholders; corporate governance practices substitute for lack of investor protection and vice versa
De Medeiros and Da Silveira (2007)	16 banks of six Latin American countries: 2003-2005	Corporate values as measured by: ethics, corporate governance, social responsibility, sustainability, transparency	Firm size, loan ratio, loan growth, Return on Assets, leverage, beta	Stock performance as measured by: stock volatility, liquidity, abnormal stock returns	Negative and significant relationship between corporate governance values and liquidity and volatility
Ding, Zhang, and Zhang (2007)	273 privately-owned and state-owned Chinese companies: 2002	Firm's ownership concentration and different ownership types (difference between state as blockholders and private blockholders)	Total assets, leverage	Earnings management	Relationship between earnings management measures and ownership concentration a non-linear, inverted U-shape relationship known as entrenchment versus alignment effect.
Hsu (2007)	258 firms: 2003	Equity ownership structure, directors' and supervisors' structure	High and low information transparency	Firm values as measured by book values per stock, price to book ratio, stock price, P/E ratio	Information transparency influences benefits of corporate governance (equity ownership structure and directors' and supervisors' structure) which in turn enhances firm values

Table 8. Corporate Governance and the Firm: International Evidence (cont.)

Study	Sample	Corporate Governance Measures	Control Variables	Firm Value Measures	Findings
Jaggi and Tsui (2007)	1,588 observations for Hong Kong firms: 1995-1999	Independent directors	Firm size, total assets, risk, growth	Insider selling	Executives manage earnings to maximize their private benefits from insider selling; Earnings management can be reduced by independent directors when no member of the family with majority ownership is present on corporate boards as a director
Lai and Tam (2007)	-2,634 firm-year observations (2000-2002).	Independent directors	Size, and leverage	-Income-smoothing earnings	- Results suggest that Chinese firms that voluntarily adopt independent directors, as well as firms that have a larger fraction of independent directors, are more likely to reduce the practice of income smoothing.
Machuga and Teitel (2007)	92 Mexican firms	The implementation of the Mexican Corporate Governance Code	Differences in earnings variability, log of total assets, leverage, change in revenues, revenues, percentage change in total liabilities, and capital intensity defined as revenues divided by total assets.	earnings quality such as: income smoothing, timely loss recognition, and abnormal accruals, and investor confidence	Results indicated that management decreased the use of accruals to manipulate earnings after the implementation of Mexican Corporate Governance Code and therefore the quality of

Table 8. Corporate Governance and the Firm: International Evidence (cont.)

Study	Sample	Corporate Governance Measures	Control Variables	Firm Value Measures	Findings
McIntyre, Murphy, and Mitchell (2007)	151 firms: 2003	Key board composition variables (experience, team size, age, team tenure)	Firm size, CEO duality, board composition (percent insider vs. outsider directors)	Tobin's Q, EVA, ROA	Key board composition variables (high levels of experience, appropriate team size, moderate levels of variation in age and team tenure) are associated with firm performance
Sánchez-Ballesta and García-Meca (2007)	64 Spanish non-financial companies: 1999-2002	Ownership structure	Unobservable firm heterogeneity, systematic risk (market model beta), growth opportunities, earnings variability, firm size, leverage	Discretionary accruals, and informativeness of earnings	Non-linear relationship between insider ownership and discretionary accruals and between insider ownership and earnings explanatory power for returns
Alexakis, Balios, Papagelis, and Xanthakis (2006)	30 stocks: 9-24-1999 to 2-11-2004	After enforcement of corporate governance legislation in Greece	Stock volatility, risk, total assets (size)	Stock returns	Stock volatility was reduced after enforcement of corporate governance codes

Table 8. Corporate Governance and the Firm: International Evidence (cont.)

Study	Sample	Corporate Governance Measures	Control Variables	Firm Value Measures	Findings
Shen and Chih (2007)	495 companies: April 2001 - February 2002	Firm-level governance data	Firm performance	Earnings management, financial ratios	Firms with good corporate governance tend to have less earnings management; large firms more likely to smooth earnings, but good corporate governance mitigated this behavior; firms with higher growth more likely to engage in earnings smoothing and earnings aggressiveness, but good corporate governance mitigated this effect
Niu (2006)	519 firm-year observations for the accrual model and 528 firm-year observations for the returns-earnings association model: 2001-2004	Board composition, management shareholding, shareholders' rights, extent of disclosure of governance practices	Operating cash flow, firm performance, auditor specialization, firm size, leverage	Accounting-based measure of earnings management and market-based measure of earnings informativeness	Governance quality negatively associated with level of abnormal accruals (corporate governance proxy) and positively influenced return-earnings association
Rahman and Ali (2006)	97 firms in Malaysia Bursa: 2002-2003	Board directors, audit committee, concentrated ownership	Firm size, risk, performance	Earnings management	Positive association between size of board of directors and earnings management; association between the other two corporate governance mechanisms (independence of board and audit committee) and earnings management was not significant

Table 8. Corporate Governance and the Firm: International Evidence (cont.)

Study	Sample	Corporate Governance Measures	Control Variables	Firm Value Measures	Findings
Shen, Hsu, and Chen (2006)	67 firms: 1990-1992	Ownership ratio of board of directors and supervisors, managerial ownership, institutional ownership ratio, and ratio of pledged stocks held by board of directors and supervisors	None	Firm values as measured by net present value per stock, stock price, book value per stock ratio, price-earnings ratio	Significant positive relationship between ownership ratio of board of directors and book value per share: Institutional ownership ratios had no relationships with price earnings ratio
Ting (2006)	207 IPO companies listed in Taiwan Security Exchange: 1992-2002	Entrenchment effect and corporate governance	Leverage and size	Market-based performance (total returns) and accounting-based performance (EPS, ROA, and ROE)	Corporate governance mechanisms add value to firm when executives realize its importance
Filatotchev, Lien, and Piesse (2005)	228 firms in Taiwan: 1999	Ownership structure and board characteristics	Industry effects and resource allocation factors	Accounting ratios, sales per issued capital, earnings per share, market-to-book ratio	Presence of institutional ownership, foreign financial institution, and family ownership and control are associated with better firm performance

Table 8. Corporate Governance and the Firm: International Evidence (cont.)

Study	Sample	Corporate Governance Measures	Control Variables	Firm Value Measures	Findings
Bauer, Gunster and Otten (2004)	249-269 firms: 2000-2001	Two portfolios of poor versus well-governed firms	Firm's book value of assets, firm age, ROE in current and previous year	Net-Profit-Margin, ROE, Tobin's Q, stock returns	No association between these governance standards and firm performance measures
DeFond and Hung (2004)	21,483 firm-year observations in 33 countries	Corporate governance offered by law and enforced by legal institutions	Cross country variations in CEO turnover, capital market development, legal origin, firm size, large blockholders and public opinion pressure on CEO turnover sensitivity	Identifying and terminating poorly performing CEOs	Strong law enforcement institutions significantly improve association between CEO turnover and poor performance; Extensive investor protection laws do not; Countries with strong law enforcement have CEO turnover that is more likely to be associated with poor stock returns when stock prices are more informative
Drobetz, Schillhofer, and Zimmermann (2004)	91 firms: 2000	30 governance proxies divided into 5 variables: Corporate governance commitment, Shareholder rights, Transparency, Management and supervisory board matters, and Auditing	Market capitalization and future growth	Expected stock returns (historical returns, dividend yield), firm valuation (Tobin's Q, market-to-book ratio)	Firms with better corporate governance are highly correlated with better operating performance, higher stock returns, and higher market valuation

Table 8. Corporate Governance and the Firm: International Evidence (cont.)

Study	Sample	Corporate Governance Measures	Control Variables	Firm Value Measures	Findings
Judge, Naoumova and Koutzevol (2003)	113 firms: December 2002	CEO duality	Firm size, ownership stake	Firm performance in Russia	Negative relationship between 'informal' CEO duality and firm performance; the more firms aggressively apply retrenchment strategy, the more negative the relationship between insider directors and firm performance
Hiraki, Hideaki, Ito, Kuroki, and Masuda (2003)	9334 firm years: 1985-1998	Main bank, intercorporate shareholding, managerial ownership	Firms that belong to the six major financial keiretsu groups, foreign ownership, R&D, advertising	Firm value in Japan	One-way ownership by banks positively related to firm value; one-way ownership by non-financial corporation was positively related to firm value; managerial ownership was monotonically and positively related to firm value
Fan and Wong (2002)	977 companies in seven East Asian economies	Ownership structure	Firm size, market to book assets, leverage, industry, specifications of earnings and stock returns	Earnings informativeness as measured by returns-earnings association	High ownership concentration is associated with low earnings informativeness; results more generalizable to other parts of world because the concentrated corporate ownership in East Asia is more representative of corporate structures throughout the world (compared to ownership in US and UK)

Table 8. Corporate Governance and the Firm: International Evidence (cont.)

Study	Sample	Corporate Governance Measures	Control Variables	Firm Value Measures	Findings
Mitton (2002)	398 firms: 1997-1998	Firm-level corporate governance	Size, leverage, country, industry	Stock price performance	Companies offering higher disclosure quality, greater transparency, a more favorable ownership structure, and a more focused organization appeared to provide greater protection to their minority shareholders during the financial crisis
Pajuste (2002)	Firms in nine Central and Eastern European (CEE) countries: June 1994 – June 2001	Rule of law, enforcement, minority shareholder protection	None	Stock returns and liquidity	The enforcement of law matters more than the quality of law; protection of minority shareholders (legal index) has a significant impact on market activity, measured by market turnover to market capitalization ratio
Volpin (2002)	205 firms: 1986-1997	Determinants of executive turnover	Size, performance	Firm valuation as a function of ownership, control structure	Direct evidence on the performance of corporate governance in a country characterized by low legal protection for investors, firms with large controlling shareholders, and some separation of ownership

Table 8. Corporate Governance and the Firm: International Evidence (cont.)

Study	Sample	Corporate Governance Measures	Control Variables	Firm Value Measures	Findings
Dahyaa, Lonie, and Power (2000)	420 firm years: 1989-1992	Boards' decisions to change composition of top management teams	Event study methodology used to isolate effect on interest	Share prices, operating profits	No share price response to the appointment or departure of senior executives; price changes were insignificant
Sarker and Sarker (2000)	1567 firms: 1995-1996	Large shareholders	Leverage, size, intangible assets, diversification, capital intensity, age effect	Firm value	Blockholdings by directors increase company value after a certain level of holdings; no evidence that institutional investors are active in governance
Kang and Shivdasani (1996)	432 Japanese firms: 1985-1990	Top management turnover	Event study used to isolate effect on interest	Stock prices	Disciplinary decisions of Japanese governance mechanisms were consistent with shareholder wealth maximization

Rahman and Ali (2006) investigate the effects of board directors, audit committee, and concentrated ownership in reducing earnings management. This study is important to the Malaysia stock market because it is an emerging multiracial society market and characterized by concentrated shareholders. Also, Malaysia was exposed to the 1997 economic crisis that weakened its corporate governance structure. However, the issuance of the Malaysian Code of Corporate Governance (2000) and the Bursa Malaysia Revamped Listing Requirement (2001) refreshed the importance of corporate governance and disclosure requirements. Therefore, a study of the effect of these changes on earnings management is important. The authors used a sample of 97 firms in the Malaysia Bursa over the period 2002-2003. The findings suggest a positive association between the size of the board of directors and earnings management. The result of the association between the other two corporate governance mechanisms (independence of board and audit committee) and earnings management was not significant.

As we consider the results that are reported in these international studies of corporate governance, it appears that firms with good corporate governance tend to have less earnings management. Further, large firms are more likely to smooth earnings, but good corporate governance mitigates this behavior. Firms with higher growth are more likely to engage in earnings smoothing and earnings aggressiveness, but again, good corporate governance mitigates this effect.

REFERENCES

Alexakis, C., Balios, D., Papagelis, G., and Xanthakis, M. 2006. An empirical investigation of the visible effects of corporate governance: The case of Greece. *Managerial Finance* 32 (8): 673-684.

Ariff, A., Ibrahim, M., and Othman, R. 2007. Determinants of firm level governance: Malaysian evidence. *Corporate Governance* 7 (5): 562-573.

Bauer, R., Gunster, N., and Otten, R. 2004. Empirical evidence on corporate governance in Europe: The effect on stock returns, firm value and performance. *Journal of Asset Management* 5: 91–104.

Cornell, B. 2003. The information that boards really need. *MIT Sloan Management Review* 44 (3): 71-76.

Cornelius, P. 2005. Good corporate practices in poor corporate governance systems: Some evidence from the global competitive report. *Corporate Governance* 5 (3): 12-23.

Dahyaa, J., Lonie, A., and Power, D. 2000. Changes in corporate management: Do they have an impact on share prices and company earnings? *Managerial Finance* 26 (9): 66-79.

Dargenidou, C., McLeay, S., and Raonic, I. 2007. Ownership, investor protection and earnings expectations. *Journal of Business Finance & Accounting* 34 (1/2): 247–268.

DeFond, M. and Hung, M. 2004. Investor protection and corporate governance: Evidence from worldwide CEO turnover. *Journal of Accounting Research* 42 (2): 269- 312.

De Medeiros, O. and Da Silveira, M. 2007. Corporate values and stock performance of Latin American banks. Available at SSRN, http://ssrn.com/abstract=958897.

Ding, Y., Zhang, H., and Zhang, J. 2007. Private vs. state ownership and earnings management: Evidence from Chinese listed companies. *Corporate Governance* 15 (2): 223-238.

Drobetz, W., Schillhofer, A., and Zimmermann, H. 2004. Corporate governance and expected stock returns: Evidence from Germany. *European Financial Management* 10 (2): 267-293.

Ezzamel, M., and Watson, R., 1997. Wearing two hats: The conflicting control and management role of nonexecutive directors. In: Keasey, F. et al. (Eds.), Corporate Governance, Economic, Management and Financial Issues. Oxford University Press.

Fan, J. and Wong, T. 2002. Corporate ownership structure and the informativeness of accounting earnings in East Asia. *Journal of Accounting & Economics* 33: 401-425.

Filatotchev, I., Lien, Y., and Piesse, J. 2005. Corporate governance and performance in publicly listed, family-controlled firms: Evidence from Taiwan. *Asia Pacific Journal of Management* 22: 257–283.

Gillan, S. and Starks, L. 2000. Corporate governance proposals and shareholder activism: The role of institutional investors. *Journal of Financial Economics* 57: 275-305.

Heracleous, L. 2001. What is the impact of corporate governance on organisational performance? *Corporate Governance* 9: 165-173.

Hiraki, T., Hideaki I., Ito, A., Kuroki, F. and Masuda, H. 2003. Corporate governance and firm value in Japan: Evidence from 1985 to 1998. *Pacific-Basin Finance Journal* 11 (3): 239-265.

Hsu, C. 2007. The influence of dimensions of corporate governance on firm values using an applied Structural Equation Model. *Journal of American Academy of Business, Cambridge* 11 (1): 204-213.

Jaggi, B. and Tsui, J. 2007. Insider trading, earnings management and corporate governance: Empirical evidence based on Hong Kong firms. *Journal of International Financial Management and Accounting* 18 (3): 192-222.

Judge, W., Naoumova, I., and Koutzevol, N. 2003. Corporate governance and firm performance in Russia: An empirical study. *Journal of World Business* 38: 385-396.

Kang, J. and Shivdasani, A. 1996. Does the Japanese governance system enhance shareholder wealth? Evidence from the stock-price effects of top management turnover. *Review of Financial Studies* 9 (4): 1061-1095.

Koehn, D. and Ueng, J. 2005. Evaluating the evaluators: Should investors trust corporate governance metrics ratings? *Journal of Management and Governance* 9: 111–128.

Lai, L. and Tam, H. 2007. Independent directors and the propensity to smooth earnings: A study of corporate governance in China. *The Business Review, Cambridge* 7(1):328-335.

Machuga, S. and Teitel, K. 2007. The effects of the Mexican corporate governance code on quality of earnings and its components. *Journal of International Accounting Research* 6 (1): 37–55.

McGunagle, D. 2007. Corporate governance in China. *The Business Review, Cambridge* 8 (1): 52-60.

McIntyre, M., Murphy, S., and Mitchell, P. 2007. The top team: Examining board composition and firm performance. *Corporate Governance* 7 (5): 547-561.

Mitton, T. 2002. A cross-firm analysis of the impact of corporate governance on the East Asian financial crisis. *Journal of Financial Economics* 64: 215-241.

Pajuste, A. 2002. Corporate governance and stock market performance in Central and Eastern Europe: A study of nine countries, 1994-2001. *Working paper 22, Centre for the Study of Economic and Social Change in Europe*.

Rahman, A. and Ali, F. 2006. Board, audit committee, culture and earnings management: Malaysian evidence. *Managerial Auditing Journal* 21 (7): 783-804.

Sánchez-Ballesta, J. and García-Meca, E. 2007. Ownership structure, discretionary accruals and the informativeness of earnings. *Corporate Governance* 15 (4): 677-691.

Sarkar, J. and Sarkar, S. 2000. Large shareholder activism in corporate governance in developing countries: Evidence from India. *International Review of Finance* 1 (3): 161-194.

Shen, C. and Chih, H. 2007. Earnings management and corporate governance in Asia's emerging markets. *Corporate Governance* 15 (5): 999-1021.

Shen, M., Hsu, C., and Chen, M. 2006. A study of ownership structures and firm values under corporate governance-the case of listed and OTC companies in Taiwan's finance industry. *Journal of American Academy of Business, Cambridge* 8 (1):184-191.

Ting, H. 2006. When does corporate governance add value? *The Business Review, Cambridge* 5 (2): 196-203.

Volpin, P. 2002. Governance with poor investor protection: Evidence from top executive turnover in Italy. *Journal of Financial Economics* 64: 61-90.

Part V.
Directions for Future Research

Chapter 11

PROACTIVE CORPORATE GOVERNANCE AND THE GLOBAL FINANCIAL CRISIS

"When the music stops, in terms of liquidity, things will be complicated. But as long as the music is playing, you've got to get up and dance. We're still dancing."

Famous Quote by Citigroup CEO: Chuck Prince - Financial Times, July 9, 2007

Obviously the music has stopped for Citigroup and other world famous firms with the onset of the global financial crisis. So, what is the solution? How might the most efficient corporate governance systems make the music play again? Recall that the main purpose of corporate governance is to 'restore the trust of investors after fraud.' However, restoring the trust of investors is most likely a long-term endeavor that requires a considerable amount of effort and collaboration among the participants in the capital and debt markets – including regulators, policy makers, investors, and various stakeholders. Investors want *credible* and *accurate* information from financial statements and other announcements made by management regarding firm performance and future expectations. That is, investors want the ability to *predict* future earnings and management behaviors (reduced uncertainty about the business environment). Simply stated, trust in business means a level of confidence regarding current and future investments based on the ability to envision the future performance of the firm through information that is regularly provided by the firm.

When the current global financial crisis began in 2008, it infused a considerable level of uncertainty in markets worldwide and significantly decreased the level of trust in the predictability of future investments. However, the role of corporate governance in restoring investors' trust in the quality and credibility of financial statements has been questioned. In fact, several points of view emerged that question the ability of corporate governance to reduce uncertainties in the market. For example, proponents of corporate governance argue that corporate governance can be a factor in restoring investors' trust. On the other hand, opponents of corporate governance argue that corporate governance failed to prevent the financial crisis and suggest a more proactive role for corporate governance.

Petra (2006) identifies various legislative reforms that were designed to prevent future corporate frauds/collapses and discusses whether these reforms would have controlled the abuses that occurred in the late 1990s through 2001. The major reforms analyzed in this paper are those set by the Sarbanes-Oxley act of 2002, NYSE, AMEX, and NASD. The author focuses on three companies that collapsed (Enron Corp., WorldCom, Inc., and Global Crossing, Ltd.) and noted that the governance structures of all three of these companies met the requirements of legislative reforms. Thus, the author warns management and shareholders to focus on the substance of the reforms to make meaningful improvements to each organization's corporate governance. In so doing, the reforms could be helpful in strengthening the ability of directors to act honestly and increasing the transparency of corporate actions, which might increase shareholders confidence in management.

The renewed interest in strong corporate governance from many worldwide scholars is encouraging. For example, George (2009), a professor of management practice at Harvard Business School states that:

> "Wall Street and U.S. business have lost the country's confidence. We need leaders who build long-term shareholder value by serving customers and society. The stock market seems well on its way to recovering from the financial crisis, but a deep scar from the recession remains. Americans lack confidence in the nation's leadership to address the challenges we currently face. The Harvard Center for Public Leadership's 2009 National Leadership Index reveals that 69% of Americans think we have a leadership crisis in the country. Another 67% believe that "unless we get better leaders, the United States will decline as a nation."
>
> At the bottom of the index's ranking of confidence in leadership are Wall Street leaders, closely followed by news media, Congressional, and business leaders. It is tempting for leaders to view these dismal results as a public relations issue emanating from the economic downturn. But this is not a PR problem: It's a leadership problem.

We opened this decade with a wave of appalling leadership failures. Ken Lay and Jeff Skilling of Enron, Bernie Ebbers of WorldCom, Joseph Nacchio of Qwest, and Dennis Kozlowski of Tyco blatantly disregarded the ethical and legal responsibilities entrusted to them by their shareholders.

Imperative: Rebuild Public trust

We are closing the decade with another wave of leadership failures. Dick Fuld of Lehman, Alan Schwartz of Bear Stearns, Angelo Mozillo of Countrywide Financial, and Chuck Prince of Citigroup (C) sacrificed financial prudence for the possibility of extraordinary short-term gains. Their decisions obliterated billions of dollars of economic wealth and almost destroyed the nation's financial system.

This crisis won't be over until a new generation of leaders emerges that understands that long-term institutional stewardship and maintaining public trust are the two imperatives of 21st century leadership.

Far too many leaders fell into the trap of believing that the purpose of business is to maximize shareholder value and reap personal rewards, rather than serve customers and the society they operate in. In my experience, those that focus primarily on maximizing shareholder value—usually with a short-term focus—are more likely to wind up destroying the value they create.

A recent study of the Standard & Poor's index of 700 international stocks from 1998 to 2009 shows that only 3 of the top 15 winners are U.S. companies—Apple (AAPL), Amazon (AMZN), and Oracle (ORCL)—all headed by leaders with a long-term focus. The 5 worst U.S. stocks were AIG, Eastman Kodak (EK), Citigroup, Ford (F), and Bristol-Myers Squibb (BMY). All had leaders with a short-term focus. This list excludes GM, K-Mart, Enron, WorldCom, and Lehman because they declared bankruptcy.

Valuing Customers Builds share Prices

Long-term leaders recognize that they cannot rely upon cost-cutting, acquisitions, and other short-term moves to create sustainable value. By focusing clearly on long-term missions, values, and strategies, they earn and keep the trust of their customers, employees, and the society they serve."

Others might argue that corporate governance codes made the firm more transparent to stakeholders and hence helped unveil financial problems not customarily discoverable under conventional business control systems. Regardless, we argue that the existence of proactive corporate governance mechanisms can be helpful; however, it is not enough to avoid another financial crisis. That is, the existence of good corporate governance codes does not prevent corporate corruption, but accurate implementation in addition to the proper education of executives and stakeholders regarding the importance of corporate governance might be helpful in preventing corporate corruption.

While corporate governance "best practices" are theoretically optimal, the truthful and appropriate application of these governance codes might differ across firms. Further, corporate governance best practices might be inefficiently applied to firms, such that the potential benefits of SOX 2002, Section 406 might not be realized. This leads us to several questions: Why does corporate governance allegedly fail to prevent corporate collapse and financial crisis? Is corporate governance not an effective monitoring tool? Are we expecting too much from the board of directors of organizations regarding their oversight role? In fact, the boards of directors assume a number of important roles within the firm besides monitoring management actions. The board of directors is responsible for providing service to the firm, monitoring all firm resources, and crafting strategic plans for the firm.

Another possible factor for the perception that corporate governance is a failure is that researchers have ignored some latent variables as they analyzed the relationship between boards of directors' governance roles and firm performance. Agency theory may not capture the conflict of interest between shareholders and management. Accordingly, a *reconstructing* of how corporate governance treats the board of directors might be needed given the fact that a board of directors' primary role is not *monitoring* management but rather *maximizing* shareholders wealth. In other words, the current governance board measures do not appear to discipline management, and as a result, perhaps it is time to test alternative theoretical frameworks and theories that might help resolve the conflict of interest between management and various stakeholders (and not just shareholders).

We recommend shifting the focus on businesses leaders/managers from being short-term to be long-term oriented leaders/managers. We suggest that part of the global financial crisis, along with claims of ineffective corporate governance codes, may be attributed to the focus that business leaders/managers have on profit maximization in the short run, forgetting about long term profit and firm continuity. As we know, shareholders of a firm are primarily interested in cash flows because they are owners of a business entity whose life is presumably infinite. However, managers are employees whose primary interest is to achieve maximum short-term cash flows to maximize their compensation. A suggested alternative for boards of directors is to focus on the long term strategy of the firm rather than their role of monitoring management. By shifting the board of directors' role to maximizing shareholders wealth in the long-term, management will be forced to forfeit their short-term focus.

Another point worth mentioning is that we find most of the literature on corporate governance focused on the effectiveness of corporate governance on firm performance of "healthy" firms, ones that have no indication of financial crisis. Research on corporate governance might make the greatest positive impact if more academics focus on firms with financial problems. A suggested research stream is to study what corporate governance can do to prevent a financial crisis (for a firm, for an industry, and perhaps for a country). In other words, we encourage researchers to test the significance of governance codes on the future performance of firms that are experiencing financial distress. Further, the heavy reliance on agency theory could be problematic (Blair and Stout, 2001). Perhaps it is time to employ other competing theories to enhance our understanding of the potential outcomes of corporate governance codes to U.S. firms.

Erkens, Hung, and Matos (2010) investigate the role corporate governance plays in the financial crisis of 2007-2008. Erkens et al. (2010) argue that corporate governance intensifies the financial crisis. They investigate the relationship between firm performance and corporate governance of 31 countries that were heavily affected by the global financial crisis and find that firms with strong corporate governance (e.g., more independent directors and institutional ownership) perform worse during the financial crisis. These firms were more likely to replace their CEO. The independent boards of these firms unintentionally encouraged aggressive risk-taking behaviors of CEOs due to the fact that the CEO compensation contracts focused on annual bonuses. In other words, boards were pushing management/CEOs to achieve higher short term abnormal returns for investors without considering the type of behavior that such compensation schemes encourage. Moreover, firms with strong corporate governance experienced a sharp decline in stock returns during the financial crisis – more than that experienced by firms with poor corporate governance structures.

REFERENCES

Blair, M. and Stout, L. 2001. Corporate accountability: Director accountability and the mediating role of the corporate board. *Washington University Law Quarterly* 79: 403-447.

Erkens, D., Hung, M., and Matos, P. 2010. Corporate governance in the 2007-2008 financial crisis: Evidence from financial institutions worldwide. *AAA 2010 Management Accounting Section (MAS) Meeting Paper*. Available at SSRN: http://ssrn.com/abstract=1433515

George, B. 2009. After the crisis: Restoring trust in U.S. leaders. *Business Week*. Available at: http://www.businessweek.com/managing/content/nov2009/ca20091123_399003.htm

Petra, S. 2006. Corporate governance reforms: Fact or fiction? *Corporate Governance* 6 (2): 107-115.

Chapter 12

META ANALYSIS ON CORPORATE GOVERNANCE

Meta analysis synthesizes the quantitative results on the association between corporate governance and organizational outcomes, such as firm value and firm performance, in order to draw reliable conclusions regarding the overall effectiveness of corporate governance codes to different constituencies. For example, a meta analysis might be used to analyze the association between board characteristics and financial reporting quality in order to draw reliable conclusions regarding the overall effectiveness of board characteristics on the quality of financial reporting. Erturk, Froud, Johal and Williams (2004) argue that corporate governance became increasingly associated with disappointment, particularly by the early of the twenty first century. They attribute the disappointment in corporate governance structures to the naïve methodology employed in most of the research, which customarily ignores the importance of the political, economic and social context around governance.

Lin and Hwang (2009) meta analyze the association between audit quality, corporate governance (e.g., board of director and audit committee characteristics) and earnings management using 48 studies. Overall, they find that strong corporate governance limits earnings management. However, they find insignificant relationships between the board of directors' stock ownership, audit committee, the CEO duality, and earnings management. Therefore, they suggest that future researchers re-examine the effect of these variables on earnings management in light of the existence of moderating variables, such as country specific characteristics or time factor.

Related, Dalton, Daily, Certo, and Roengpitya (2003); Dalton, Daily, Ellstrand, and Johnson (1998); and Tosi, Werner, Katz, Gomez-Mejia (2000), among others, conduct meta analyses on the relationship between corporate governance and firm performance. Overall, they find little evidence on the usefulness of corporate governance to the firm. Dalton, Daily, Certo, and Roengpitya's (2003) analysis focuses on insider/outsider ownership and firm performance. They analyze research on all kinds of ownership equity such as CEO equity, board equity, officers and director equity, inside board equity, outside board equity, management equity, institutional equity, and blockholder equity. Dalton, Daily, Certo, and Roengpitya (2003) find scant support on agency theory. In other words, the results of their analysis indicate a weak relationship between ownership and performance. Overall, they suggest that authors adopt a substitute theory to agency theory in the analysis of ownership-performance relationship in future research.

Overall, Dalton et al. (1998) find no meaningful relationship between board composition and independence and firm financial performance. These authors note that most of the literature employs the following variables as moderators in their model: size of the firm and nature of the performance indicators (accounting vs. market-based). Moreover, they document four primary operationalizations of board composition: inside director proportion, outside director proportion, affiliated director proportion, independent /interdependent director proportion. Their analysis includes 54 (31) empirical studies on board composition (board leadership) and performance. They find little evidence supporting the notion that stronger corporate governance leads to higher firm performance.

Tosi, Werner, Katz, Gomez-Mejia (2000) conduct a meta analysis that contains 137 articles on the association between firm performance, size, and CEO pay. They find that firm size (performance) explains 40 percent (less than 5percent) of the variance in total CEO pay. However, pay sensitivity was relatively similar (4-5 percent variance explained) for both firm size and performance. This study did not account for possible moderators that might affect CEO pay, firm size, and performance. Therefore, the study is based on the assumption that moderating the relationship between governance-performance would provide more intriguing results. Nevertheless, other researchers find contrary evidence that supports the notion that corporate governance is useful to firm value and performance. Among these researchers are the following: Margolis, Elfenbein, and Walsh (2007); Rhoades, Rechner, and Sundaramurthy (2001); Wagner, Stimpert, and Fubara (1998); and Dalton, Daily, Johnson, and Ellstrand (1999). Margolis, Elfenbein, and Walsh (2007) include 192 empirical studies and find a positive association though small. In the same vein, Rhoades, Rechner, and Sundaramurthy (2001) analyze 22 studies and find a significant positive association between board independence and firm performance. They attribute the low association in prior research to a sampling error.

Wagner, Stimpert, and Fubara (1998) suggest that the relationship between insider/outsider composition and firm performance is curvilinear. Their meta analysis uses 29 studies on the association between board composition and firm performance and find a positive association between these variables. Also, Dalton, Daily, Johnson, and Ellstrand (1999) analyze board of director's size and firm performance using 131 studies and find a positive association between board size and firm performance. Consequently, one proposed avenue for future research on corporate governance is to use contingency theory as a substitute for agency theory. By utilizing contingency theory, we anticipate that a wide set of variables would enhance our understanding of the usefulness of corporate governance. For example, one can moderate for firm configurations in the governance-performance relations. Firm configurations are documented to affect firm value, according to Ketchen, Combs, Russell, Shook, Dean, Runge, Lohrke, Naumann, Haptonstahl, Baker, Bechstein, Handler, Honig, Lamoureux (1997.) Ketchen et al. (1997) analyze 40 studies on the association between firm configurations and performance. They provide evidence that organization performance is partially explained by a firm's configuration. Organizational configurations are groups of organizations sharing common characteristics. In general, the organizational configurations can be defender, prospector, analyzer, or reactor. Ketchen et al. (1997) suggest that future researcher should incorporate proxies for firm configurations in their studies that measure the firm performance. They recommend three possible moderators that would explain firm performance. These moderators are: broad definition and configurations, single-industry sample, and longitudinal designs. Another possible variable to moderate is the key board composition as suggested by McIntyre, Murphy, and Mitchell (2007). McIntyre et al. (2007) find that the key board composition variables (high levels of experience, appropriate team size, moderate levels of variation in age, and team tenure) are associated with firm performance.

Based on these meta analyses and empirical results, we can clearly observe the mixed results and ambiguity of the association between firm performance and corporate governance measures. Moreover, corporate governance practices are providing even more disappointing outcomes as we continue to observe an increasing number of corporate failures worldwide. We suggest that future research moderate for these variables in their models. Possible reasons beyond the documented mixed results involve the fact that firm performance must be measured over a long horizon and this leads to noisy data and hence mixed results (Bhagat and Black 2001). The use of OLS in the analysis produces biased estimates especially in the presence of endogenous relationships between corporate governance variables and firm performance measures.

REFERENCES

Bhagat, S. and Black, B. 2001. The non-correlation between board independence and long term firm performance. *Journal of Corporation Law* 27: 231-274.

Dalton, D., Daily, C., Certo, S., and Roengpitya, R. 2003. Meta-analyses of financial performance and equity: Fusion or confusion? *Academy of Management Journal* 46: 13-26.

Dalton, D., Daily, C., Ellstrand, A., and Johnson, J. 1998. Meta-analytic reviews of board composition, leadership structure, and financial performance. *Strategic Management Journal* 19: 269–290.

Dalton, D., Daily, C., Johnson, J., and Ellstrand, A. 1999. Number of directors and financial performance: A Meta-analysis. *The Academy of Management Journal* 42 (6): 674-686.

Erturk, I., Froud, J., Johal, S., and Williams, K. 2004. Corporate governance and disappointment. *Review of International Political Economy* 11: 677-713

Ketchen, D., Combs, J., Russell, G., Shook, C., Dean, M., Runge, J., Lohrke, F., Naumann, S., Haptonstahl, D., Baker, R., Bechstein, B., Handler, C., Honig, H., and Lamoureux, S. 1997. Organizational configurations and performance: A Meta analysis. *Academy of Management Journal* 40: 223-240.

Lin, J. and Hwang, M. 2009. Audit quality, corporate governance, and earnings management: A Meta-analysis. *International Journal of Auditing* 14 (1): 57-77.

Margolis, J., Elfenbein, H., and Walsh, J. 2007. Does it pay to be good? A Meta-analysis and redirection of research on the relationship between corporate social and financial performance. *Working paper.*

McIntyre, M., Murphy, S. and Mitchell, P. 2007. The top team: Examining board composition and firm performance. *Corporate Governance* 7 (5): 547-561.

Rhoades, D., Rechner, P., and Sundaramurthy, C. 2001. A Meta-analysis of board leadership structure and financial performance: are "two heads better than one"? *Corporate Governance* 9 (4): 311-319.

Tosi, H., Werner, S., Katz, J., and Gomez-Mejia, L. 2000. How much does performance matter? A Meta-analysis of CEO pay studies. *Journal of Management* 26 (2): 301-339.

Wagner, J., Stimpert, J., and Fubara, E. 1998. Board composition and organizational performance: Two studies of insider/outsider effects. *Journal of Management Studies* 35 (5): 655-678.

Chapter 13

ADDITIONAL RECOMMENDATIONS FOR FUTURE RESEARCH

Turnbull (1997) argues that U.S. theory of the firm became less relevant as economic transactions became more mediated by 'cultural priorities, business related associations, trade, vocational, family, social and political networks'. Accordingly, adoption of a very narrow research paradigm limits the potential contribution of corporate governance research. Reliance on archival data is common, but other methodologies and data sources might offer (or capture) important facets of corporate governance that might otherwise be overlooked. For example, we encourage researchers to build well-designed experimental studies and use relevant psychological theories that attempt to explain agency costs and implications.

Another potential topic of interest is the period surrounding mergers and acquisitions. We recommend testing the relevance of corporate governance codes to the process of mergers and acquisitions due to the fact that prior studies have documented high top management turnover during such periods. The extant literature has mainly focused on investigating CEO turnover, although the top executive team is comprised of many parties that might be equally interesting to study, such as the COO, president, vice-president, treasurer, CFO, and secretary. Investigating the top management team turnover might help build a comprehensive view on turnover issues and corporate governance.

In the next section, we group our previous recommendations into nine areas. The main purpose of these nine categories is to consolidate our recommendations of corporate governance internal and external mechanisms.

USING AGENCY THEORY OR OTHER WELL-ESTABLISHED THEORIES?

Hart (1995) criticizes agency theory for dealing with the firm as a 'black box'. Agency theory predicts that corporate governance will maximize the outputs of shareholders wealth by strengthening the governance structure (the input to the desired outcome of profit maximization). However, little is known about how the inputs are transformed into outputs. Another issue is feedback. We need to know whether the actual outputs are originated through the traditional inputs we entered into the process. In other words, we need to verify that shareholders' maximization is indeed the output of a well-developed governance structure and nothing else. Lazonick and O'Sullivan (2000) doubted the alleged relationship between maximization of shareholders value and sustainability of economic prosperity, given the performance of the U.S. economy. These authors argue that shareholder maximization may be an important target to run down a company and an economy but may not be sufficient to build up a U.S. firm and the economy.

Moreover, support for the resource dependence theory and stewardship theory suggests that the heavy focus on the board of directors' monitoring role is unjustifiable. In the same vein, Cornell (2003) suggests that despite the significant initiative in corporate governance to ensure boards' independence, the boards' needs might be different from the information offered through the adoption of corporate governance mechanisms. Boards are interested in the information contained in some basic financial tools. They simply cannot monitor the management of a firm without sufficient information. Also, directors normally meet on average four to six times a year, and they have limited time to collect the information they need to rationally carry out their responsibilities towards shareholders.

Accordingly, we encourage researchers to explore an interdisciplinary analysis based on different facets of governance tools and diverse theories. Among the analyses that can be investigated is the use of psychological theories in explaining managers and traders behavior within different corporate governance contexts. For example, Koonce (2005) believes there is a misconception among archival accounting researchers that individuals behave according to the normative model (expected utility theory) and even if any individual irrationality exists, it will be eliminated by market forces. However, the current financial crisis does not support this contention, as market forces fail to mitigate individual behavior irrationality. This is where psychology theories may prove useful because they are descriptive in nature. They tend to describe the process by which judgment and decision making occur in financial markets. Both cognitive psychology and social psychology are helpful in explaining how people think and how the environment affects the way people make decisions.

BELIEVING IN MARKET FORCES

Another proposal to get the most out of corporate governance is to believe in the force of the market. Hart (1995) discusses the Chicago-view argument that implies *"as long as the founders sell their claims in a competitive market, they will receive an amount equal to the net present value of the returns on all claims"*. If this were the case, there would be no need for a statutory corporate governance system because executives would be disciplined by market-wide forces.

It is true that the business environment has changed dramatically over the last several decades, but the solution to the problems arising from this fast changing business environment must stem from the origin of the troubles. If we conceive of the origin of the trouble as 'change', then the solution must be *dynamic* rather than *static.* In so doing, management will have the discretion they need to tailor the corporate governance structure that best fits their business environment and gives them the authority to change this governance structure as the business environment changes. Market forces, as governance tools, would be expected to take longer than regulations, such as SOX 2002, to reap the desired change in behavior. In this vein, Benz and Frey (2007) attribute the failure of corporate governance practices (in reducing agency costs) to the short-term perspective of the current governance codes. These authors suggest that corporate governance practices should be based on public governance practices, such as: fixed compensation not dependent on pay-for-performance, division of power based on democratic policies, and reliance on institutionalized competition in core areas of a firm.

Adopting Strategic Corporate Governance Codes

Another proposed improvement to get the most out of corporate governance is to broaden the limited view of corporate governance by researchers. The extant literature contains a plethora of studies based on board independence, characteristics, composition, and structure to focus on strategic roles of the board of directors. For example, Daily, Dalton, and Cannella (2003) contend that there are three promising themes that might provide an intriguing insight for future corporate governance research. These themes are: board oversight, shareholder activism, and governing firms in crisis. Heracleous (2001) calls for a strategic perspective on corporate governance that attempts to match corporate practices with the corporate governance code. We wholeheartedly endorse Heracleous's proposal to shift the focus on strategic corporate governance. Heracleous (2001) claims that corporate governance is focused on strategy ratification rather than strategy formation. Corporate governance should be tied to strategic management such as diversification, resource management, and strategic change, mainly because of well-established evidence on the association between strategic management and higher firm performance (Heracleous 2001.)

Striving to Give Priority to Proactive Corporate Governance Codes

The value of corporate governance is a controversial topic in both literature and practice. Prior research suggests that good corporate governance adds value to shareholders' wealth, protects investors, increases the ratio of returns, affects sources of financing for firms, and identifies and terminates poorly performing CEOs. Also, corporate governance appears to add value when corporate executives realize its importance. Future research on the value of corporate governance might investigate the following topics: (1) a comparison of the effect of top management turnover in financially healthy versus weak firms; (2) a comparison of the effect of turnover for the top management team (perhaps the CEO and the top seven to nine executives); (3) a comparison of sophisticated and unsophisticated investors regarding their ability to discern the extent or quality of corporate governance mechanisms; (4) the quality of corporate governance disclosures (amount and detail of information); and (5) a study of developing economies using Khiari's, Karaa, and Omri (2007) index. Further, we encourage researchers to focus on the need for proactive corporate governance that predicts a firm's future performance and hence provides the necessary governance mechanisms. We observe that most of the existing corporate governance codes (e.g., Sarbanes Oxley Act 2002) are passive (versus proactive) in nature and deal with a past crisis.

Using XBRL as a Governance Tool

Researchers might wish to compare governmental organizations, not-for-profit organizations, and publicly traded companies (both inter-country and intra-country) that have adopted XBRL technology. XBRL is a road ahead and not a dead end in the domain of corporate governance research. There appear to be significant benefits that can be realized from the adoption of XBRL inside the firm. We believe this line of research might offer important insights for all levels of investors, and might also be of interest to the management of these organizations, regulators, analysts, and others. Our belief is based upon a study by Hodge, Kennedy, and Maines (2004) in which the authors investigate the benefits to investors of using a search-facilitating technology. The authors find that when stock option accounting varies between firms, the use of an XBRL-enhanced search engine increased the likelihood that individuals acquired information about stock option compensation disclosed in the footnotes. They also find that XBRL helped individuals integrate the implications of the information, resulting in different investment decisions between individuals who used the technology and those that did not use the search engine.

The use of technology can facilitate the comparisons noted above. For example, the eXtensible Business Reporting Language (XBRL) was developed to improve the accuracy and reliability of financial information. Cohen, Schiavina, and Servais (2005) claim that XBRL's potential benefits include increased efficiency and transparency of financial information, which offers both opportunities and challenges for corporate governance. That is, digital reporting (documents in XBRL format) presents the opportunity for more reusable digital reports, more types of information available on a more frequent basis, improved internal reporting, and a stronger internal controls environment. The official website for XBRL information offers a substantial amount of information on this technology and also identifies the countries that have developed taxonomies for reporting certain financial reports in XBRL format. The U.S. and many other countries are participating in the XBRL consortium, including representation from governmental organizations, not-for-profit organizations, and publicly-traded companies. As of 2002, the consortium had more than 160 worldwide members (Hannon 2002).

Accordingly, researchers might wish to compare governmental organizations, not-for-profit organizations and publicly traded companies (both inter-country and intra-country) to investigate corporate governance properties of XBRL technology. For the companies and organizations that have adopted XBRL for financial reporting purposes, do they also use other important governance mechanisms? For example, do these companies and organizations also use SysTrust or WebTrust? Do they have a comprehensive online Privacy Policy, a published Code of Conduct, or other mechanisms that improve the level of corporate governance? What is the association between these mechanisms? Are some of these mechanisms synergistic? Is there an association between these mechanisms and the quality (or level) of financial reporting transparency (quality and quantity of information)?

Within the context of XBRL, future research might focus on the association between specific components of financial statements and corporate governance mechanisms to promote financial reporting quality. Specifically, as the marketplace continues to become more interconnected, researchers might focus on the financial statements components to discern important differences (or similarities) across these components with respect to the corporate governance mechanisms that are in place. Additional governance research is encouraged to explore more comprehensively the use of financial accounting information in additional corporate control mechanisms.

Documenting Corporate Governance Codes by Historians

Although the extant body of literature on corporate governance is substantial, we believe that corporate governance will continue to be an important area for future research for a number of reasons. First, corporate accounting scandals, failures, and financial statement restatements continue to shake the confidence of investors in the worldwide capital markets. As a result, regulators and legislators become involved. Second, the continued improvement of technologies (such as XBRL) will make financial information more readily available. Third, the recent global financial crisis is an extraordinary economic event that attracts worldwide attention on the public interest. Moreover, this global financial crisis pinpoints the role corporate governance plays or should play in curbing future financial crises. Accordingly, as transparency of financial information increases, those inside and outside of organizations will have greater access to more types of digital information on a more frequent basis. In addition, increased transparency of financial information should dispel the fiscal illusion that has prevented analysts, investors, and other interested outside parties from accurately and comprehensively evaluating corporate financial statements.

We support Daily, Dalton, and Cannella's (2003) call for making corporate governance codes part of U.S. history. This rich volume of research over the last 25 years is sufficient evidence that corporate governance became a 'tradition' in the U.S. business environment. Corporate governance codes, consequences, and even the mysterious global financial crisis following a series of governance provisions should be documented in U.S. history. Successive business leaders, researchers, and students should be aware of what happened and understand the lessons that may be learned regarding corporate governance.

We note that corporate governance codes are mostly cited and discussed by academics and some of the professional experts such as economists and lawyers, but not by historians. We believe that corporate governance has become part of the U.S. culture and an inevitable experience to successive business generations. One of our recommendations also is to include corporate governance codes in school curriculums as part of the learning process. Students should be made aware of corporate governance mechanisms that help to curb corruption and fraud. They need to understand how such mechanisms contribute to a healthy economy and to national stability.

Working towards Corporate Governance Convergence

The results of Gugler, Muller, Yurtoglu's (2003) study suggest that the strength of corporate governance systems can make a difference in a firm's sources of finance for investment and in the returns on investments. These authors use the nature of a country's legal system and its level of development as two criteria to measure the strength of a country's corporate governance system. The sample included 19,010 companies for 46 countries for the time period 1985 to 2001. The authors report stronger corporate governance systems in developed countries relative to developing countries. The authors also find that in countries with strong (weak) corporate governance, the average ratio of the returns on a company's total investment to its cost of capital was greater (less) than one. The authors claimed that laws and regulations covering corporate governance were much more rigorous in developed countries than in developing countries where law enforcement agencies are often under-funded and their personnel are much more willing to accept bribes.

The main purpose of Shleifer and Vishny's (1997) study is to examine the importance of legal protection of investors and of ownership concentration in corporate governance systems around the world. The United States, Germany, Japan, and the United Kingdom appear to have some of the best corporate governance systems in the world, and the differences between them are probably small relative to their differences from other countries. For example, Italian corporate governance mechanisms are so undeveloped as to substantially retard the flow of external capital to firms. In less developed countries, including some of the transition economies, corporate governance mechanisms are practically nonexistent. In Russia, the weakness of corporate governance mechanisms leads to substantial diversion of assets by managers of many privatized firms, and the virtual nonexistence of external capital supply to firms. Corporate governance systems in most other countries, ranging from poor developing countries, to transition economies, to some rich European countries, lack certain essential elements of a good system. In most cases, countries lack mechanisms for legal protection of investors.

Klapper and Love (2002) claim that cross-country differences in laws and their enforcement affect ownership structure, dividend payout, availability and cost of external finance, and market valuations. For example, firms could improve investor protection rights by using a number of tools such as: increasing disclosure, selecting well-functioning and independent boards, imposing disciplinary mechanisms to prevent management and controlling shareholders from engaging in expropriation of minority shareholders, etc. The final sample in this study is 374 firms in 14 countries – Brazil, Chile, Hong Kong, India, Indonesia, Korea, Malaysia, Pakistan, Philippines, Singapore, South Africa, Taiwan, Thailand, and Turkey. The authors use data from a report by Credit Lyonnais Securities Asia (CLSA) that constructed corporate governance rankings for 495 firms across 25 emerging markets and 18 sectors. The authors find that firms in countries with weak overall legal systems have, on average, lower governance rankings. The authors also find that firm-level governance was correlated with variables related to the extent of the asymmetric information and contracting imperfections that firms face, while good governance was positively correlated with market valuation and operating performance (stronger relationship in countries with weaker legal systems). The authors argue that firm-level corporate governance matters more in countries with weak shareholder protection and poor judicial efficiency. Nevertheless, they do not support the view that firm-level corporate governance is a replacement for country-level judicial reform. Their results suggest that firms can reduce their cost of capital by establishing credible investor protection provisions through using provisions in their charters to improve their corporate governance, which may improve their performance and valuation.

These studies lead to additional suggestions for research. In particular, understanding the differences among corporate governance structures within the world's leading economies is important to justify, facilitate, and enrich the transfer of capital and listing in stock exchanges among these economies. As hard as the International Financial Reporting Standards' (IFRS) convergence sounds, we expect the convergence of corporate governance codes to face the same resistance, problems, and efforts faced by regulators of IFRS. To reduce problems associated with the convergence of corporate governance codes, we recommend research around the idea of forming a world-governance committee to address these issues and work on achieving both short and long term worldwide governance agendas. Lessons, cases, governance tools, and agendas could be studied and documented to help improve governance mechanisms for future generations.

STUDYING ANTECEDENTS, CHARACTERISTICS, AND CONSEQUENCES OF CORPORATE GOVERNANCE ENDOGENOUS STRUCTURE

Anecdotal evidence suggests a causal effect of corporate governance on U.S. firm's outcomes, such as: firm performance, stock price performance, financial reporting quality, cost of capital and firm value. However, we cannot rule out the reverse causality hypothesis. In other words, firm value and performance measures might impact the effectiveness of corporate governance structures, and hence, the effectiveness of the U.S. firm. Leuz, Nanda, and

Wysocki (2003) suggest an endogenous relationship between corporate governance and financial reporting quality, measured by earnings management (e.g., loss avoidance and income smoothing). They suggest that the level of investor protection may curb insiders from manipulating earnings. They find that countries with strong investor protections are less likely to manage earnings.

We find that researchers are controlling for the endogenous relationship between governance and firm performance in their empirical models with no explanation for why endogenous exists in the first place. We encourage future research to explore this missing link in corporate governance research to enrich our understanding on the usefulness of corporate governance to the firm. In fact, understanding the mechanisms of the endogenous structure of the governance-performance model is crucial in obtaining the most benefit from corporate governance codes.

Conclusion

Researchers have not yet calculated the bottom line or the net value of the Sarbanes Oxley Act of 2002 or other regulations issued by the SEC or the NYSE. Researchers also have not experimentally tested the pervasiveness of market competition forces as a natural (*presumably* costless) governance tool. Future research is still needed to enhance our understanding of the association between corporate governance and firm value, performance, and the overall economy. Researchers are encouraged to utilize interdisplinary approaches that take into account various facets of the U.S. and non-U.S. economies, disciplines, users with diverse interests (e.g. stakeholders instead of focusing solely on shareholders), and managers behaviors under different theoretical frameworks (e.g., stewardship theory, contingent theory, resource dependence theory, or a mix of some of these theories). We suggest that future research adopt the perspective that U.S. regulators, legislators, and market participants want better corporate governance systems (Holmstrom and Kaplan 2003).

Holmstrom and Kaplan (2003) demonstrate that U.S. corporate scandals did not preclude the U.S. stock market from outperforming those of world markets. By the same token, Aggarwal, Erel, Stulz, and Williamson (2007) compare the corporate governance systems of the U.S. with those in foreign firms. Aggarwal et al. (2007) find that U.S. firms still have better corporate governance systems compared to the governance systems in foreign firms. To conclude, the U.S. stock market and economy are still the largest, most organized, and least corrupt systems among the world's markets and economies. U.S. business leaders, regulators, legislators, and market participants are very quick yet efficient in addressing corporate governance mechanisms that failed to reduce agency costs.

REFERENCES

Aggarwal, R., Erel, I., Stulz, R., and Williamson, R. 2007. Do U.S. firms have the best corporate governance? A cross-country examination of the relation between corporate governance and shareholder wealth. *NBER working paper 12819.*

Benz, M. and Frey, B. 2007. Corporate governance: What can we learn from public governance? *Academy of Management Review* 32 (1): 92-104.

Cohen, E., Schiavina, T., and Servais, O. 2005. XBRL: The standardised business language for 21st century reporting and governance. *International Journal of Disclosure and Governance* 2 (4): 368-394.

Cornell, B. 2003. The information that boards really need. *MIT Sloan Management Review* 44 (3): 71-76.

Daily, C., Dalton, D. and Cannella, A. 2003. Corporate governance: Decades of dialogue and data. *Academy of Management Review* 28: 371-382.

Extensible Business Reporting Language (XBRL) web page: www.xbrl.org.

Gugler, K., Mueller, D., and Yurtoglu, B. 2003. Corporate governance and the returns on investment. *ECGI Finance Working Paper No. 06/2003*. Available at SSRN, http://ssrn.com/abstract=299520.

Hannon, N. 2002. Accounting scandals: Can XBRL help? *Strategic Finance* (August): 61–62.

Hart, O. 1995. Corporate governance: Some theory and implications. *The Economic Journal* 105 (430): 678-689.

Heracleous, L. 2001. What is the impact of corporate governance on organizational performance? *Corporate Governance* 9 (3): 165-173.

Hodge, F., Kennedy, S., and Maines, L. 2004. Recognition versus disclosure in financial statements: Does search-facilitating technology improve transparency? *The Accounting Review* 79 (3): 687-703.

Holmstrom, B. and Kaplan, S. 2003. The State of U.S. Corporate Governance: What's Right and What's Wrong? *ECGI - Finance Working Paper No. 23/2003*. Available at SSRN: http://ssrn.com/abstract=441100

Khiari, W., Karaa, A., and Omri, A. 2007. Corporate governance efficiency: An indexing approach using the stochastic frontier analysis. *Corporate Governance* 7 (2): 148-161.

Klapper, L. and Love, I. 2002. Corporate governance, investor protection, and performance in emerging markets. *World Bank Policy Research Working Paper 2818*.

Koonce, L. and Mercer, M. 2005. Using psychology theories in archival financial accounting research. *McCombs Research Paper Series No. ACC-01-05*. Available at SSRN: http://ssrn.com/abstract=311105

Lazonick, W. and O'Sullivan, M. 2000. Maximizing shareholder value: a new ideology for corporate governance. *Economy and Society* 29 (1): 13-35.

Leuz, C., Nanda, N., and Wysocki, P. 2003. Earnings management and investor protection: an international comparison. *Journal of Financial Economics* 69: 505-27.

Shleifer, A. and Vishny, R. 1997. A survey of corporate governance. *The Journal of Finance* LII (2): 737-783.

Turnbull, S. 1997. Corporate Governance: its scope, concerns and theories. *Corporate Governance* 5 (4): 180-206.

INDEX

D

E

F

G

H

I

J

K

L

M

N

O

P

Q

R

S

T